CAMBRIDGE LIBR

Books of enduring

Travel and Exploration

The history of travel writing dates back to the Bible, Caesar, the Vikings and the Crusaders, and its many themes include war, trade, science and recreation. Explorers from Columbus to Cook charted lands not previously visited by Western travellers, and were followed by merchants, missionaries, and colonists, who wrote accounts of their experiences. The development of steam power in the nineteenth century provided opportunities for increasing numbers of 'ordinary' people to travel further, more economically, and more safely, and resulted in great enthusiasm for travel writing among the reading public. Works included in this series range from first-hand descriptions of previously unrecorded places, to literary accounts of the strange habits of foreigners, to examples of the burgeoning numbers of guidebooks produced to satisfy the needs of a new kind of traveller - the tourist.

Sir Francis Drake

The publications of the Hakluyt Society (founded in 1846) made available edited (and sometimes translated) early accounts of exploration. The first series, which ran from 1847 to 1899, consists of 100 books containing published or previously unpublished works by authors from Christopher Columbus to Sir Francis Drake, and covering voyages to the New World, to China and Japan, to Russia and to Africa and India. Volume 4 was edited by William Desborough Cooley, one of the founders of the Society, who stressed the importance of historical accounts to modern exploration. First published in 1849, it contains the eye-witness account by Thomas Maynarde of Sir Francis Drake's last voyage across the Atlantic (1595-6) and his failed attack on San Juan in Puerto Rico, together with a Spanish account of the attack, and an English translation. The text is accompanied by explanatory notes.

Cambridge University Press has long been a pioneer in the reissuing of out-of-print titles from its own backlist, producing digital reprints of books that are still sought after by scholars and students but could not be reprinted economically using traditional technology. The Cambridge Library Collection extends this activity to a wider range of books which are still of importance to researchers and professionals, either for the source material they contain, or as landmarks in the history of their academic discipline.

Drawing from the world-renowned collections in the Cambridge University Library, and guided by the advice of experts in each subject area, Cambridge University Press is using state-of-the-art scanning machines in its own Printing House to capture the content of each book selected for inclusion. The files are processed to give a consistently clear, crisp image, and the books finished to the high quality standard for which the Press is recognised around the world. The latest print-on-demand technology ensures that the books will remain available indefinitely, and that orders for single or multiple copies can quickly be supplied.

The Cambridge Library Collection will bring back to life books of enduring scholarly value (including out-of-copyright works originally issued by other publishers) across a wide range of disciplines in the humanities and social sciences and in science and technology.

Sir Francis Drake

His Voyage, 1595

Thomas Maynarde
Edited by
William Desborough Cooley

CAMBRIDGE UNIVERSITY PRESS

Cambridge, New York, Melbourne, Madrid, Cape Town, Singapore,
São Paolo, Delhi, Dubai, Tokyo, Mexico City

Published in the United States of America by Cambridge University Press, New York

www.cambridge.org
Information on this title: www.cambridge.org/9781108008013

This edition first published 1849
This digitally printed version 2010

ISBN 978-1-108-00801-3 Paperback

WORKS ISSUED BY

The Hakluyt Society.

SIR FRANCIS DRAKE

HIS VOYAGE,

1595.

M.DCCC.XLIX.

SIR FRANCIS DRAKE

HIS VOYAGE,

1595,

BY

THOMAS MAYNARDE,

TOGETHER WITH THE

SPANISH ACCOUNT OF DRAKE'S ATTACK ON PUERTO RICO.

EDITED, FROM THE ORIGINAL MANUSCRIPTS,

BY

W. D. COOLEY.

LONDON:

PRINTED FOR THE HAKLUYT SOCIETY.

M.DCCC.XLIX.

THE HAKLUYT SOCIETY.

Council.

PREFACE.

The name of Sir Francis Drake is one of the brightest ornaments of Hakluyt's collection; and a Society, which undertakes to continue and complete the labours of the latter, cannot certainly be better employed than in publishing documents illustrating the life and achievements of that distinguished seaman.

In conformity with this view, the two original pieces which follow have been selected for publication; both brief but full of life, and the first of them, in particular, very racy and characteristic.

The value of Maynarde's paper (additional MSS., No. 5209, in the library of the British Museum), lies in the writer's intimacy with Sir Francis Drake, whom he accompanied in the unfortunate expedition which is the subject of the following narrative, and in the shrewdness of his remarks, clothed occasionally in the quaintest language. It cannot be denied that it tends to dispel much of the romance which has hitherto coloured so brilliantly the history of the naval hero. But truth is thereby a gainer. Romance elevates the hero at the expense of human nature, and sacrifices the many for the glory of one. It may not be without advantage to learn, from the example of one so justly celebrated as Drake, what sordid motives may be cloaked under the pretence of national glory, and how mistrustfully we ought to listen to the professedly generous instigators of war and rapine.

The Spanish paper, Relacion de lo Sucedido, etc., (additional MSS. No. 13,964, British Museum), which has the form of an official report, or dispatch, is extremely interesting, inasmuch as it allows us to see, in immediate juxtaposition and direct contrast, the accounts of the affair at Puerto Rico, as given by the two belligerent parties.

These papers are here reproduced from the originals without change or emendation ; so that their defects, whether attributable to negligence or ignorance, may be taken into consideration in estimating their intrinsic worth.

The superficial inaccuracies of Maynarde's paper are not a few; his constant misspelling of proper names, as Corasaw for Curaçoa, St. Tomarta for Sta. Martha, would seem to prove him illiterate. It is still more important, that, through oversight and omission, he states the number of the forces, who marched from Nombre de Dios to attack Panama, to be fifty, instead of seven hundred and fifty.

It is amusing to observe the variance between the Spanish and English accounts of the same action, both written in good faith. The Spaniards had but seventy guns, and yet the English reckoned 5160 pieces of artillery playing on them. This tremendous fire would appear from the English account to have done no great harm, while the Spaniards allege that they killed four hundred of the enemy, besides wounding many more.

But this is not the place for a critical examination of the following pages. The conflicting statements and opinions respecting the closing scene of Drake's eventful life, are amply detailed in Mr. Barrow's justly popular volume. Here it will be sufficient to observe that Maynarde's keen and natural comments on his commanders, proceed from one who, in regard to Drake, certainly writes in a friendly spirit, and from whom the truth was wrung by the circumstances of his situation.

W. D. C.

SIR FRANCIS DRAKE

HIS VOYAGE,

1595:

BY

THOMAS MAYNARDE.

SIR FRANCIS DRAKE

HIS VOYAGE,

1595.

It appears by the attempts and knowen purposes of the Spaniarde, as by his greedy desire to bee our neighboure in Bretaine, his fortifienge upon the river of Brest, to gaine so near us a quiet and safe rode for his fleet, his carelessness in losinge the strongehouldes and townes which he possessed in the Lowe Countries, not followinge those warres in that heate which he wonted, the rebellious rysinge of the Earle of Tyrone (wrought or drawen thereto undoubtedly by his wicked practises), that hee leaveth no means unattempted which he judged might bee a furtherance to turne our tranquillitie into accursed thraldom; so robbinge us of that quiet peace which wee, from the hands of Her Majestie (next under God), aboundently enjoy. This his bloodthirstie desire foreseene by the wisdome of our queene and counsayle, they helde no better meanes to curbe his unjust pretenses, than by sendinge forces to invade him in that kingdome from whence hee hath feathers to flye to the toppe of his high desires; they knowing that if for two or three yeeres a blowe were given him there, that might hinder the coming into Spaine of his treasure; his povertie, by reason of his daily huge payments, would be so great, and his men of warre, most of them mercenaries, that assuredly would fall from him, so woulde he have more neede of meanes to keepe his owne territories, than he nowe hath of superfluitie to thruste into others rights.

This invasion was spoken of in June 1594, a longe time before it was put in execution; and it beinge partly resolved on, Sir Francis Drake was named generall in November folowinge:—a man of greate spirit and fitt to undertake matters: in my poore opinion, better able to conduct forces and discreetly to governe in conductinge them to places where service was to be done, than to comande in the execution thereof. But, assuredly, his very name was a great terror to the enemie in all those partes, havinge heretofore done many thinges in those countries to his honorable fame and profitt. But entringe into them as the childe of fortune, it may be his selfe-willed and peremptorie comand was doubted, and that caused Her Majestie, as should seeme, to joyne Sir John Hawkins in equall commission:—a man oulde and warie, entering into matters with so laden a foote, that the other's meat woulde be eaten before his spit could come to the fire: men of so different natures and dispositions, that what the one desireth the other would commonly oppose against; and though their warie cariages sequestred it from meaner wittes, yet was it apparently seen to better judgements before our going from Plymouth, that whom the one loved, the other smaly esteemed. Agreeing best, for what I could conjecture, in giving out a glorious title to their intended jorneye, and in not so well victualinge the navie as, I deeme, was Her Majestie's pleasure it shoulde bee, both of them served them to goode purpose, for, from this havinge the distributinge of so great sommes, their miserable providinge for us would free them from incurringe any greate losse, whatsoever befel of the jorney. And the former drewe unto them so greate repaire of voluntaries[1] that they had choice to discharge suche fewe as they had

[1] Influx of volunteers.

pressed, and to enforce the staye of others who gladly would be partakers of their voyage. But notwithstandinge matters were very forward, and that they had drawen together three thousand men, and had ready furnished twenty-seven shippes, whereof six were Her Majestie's, yet many times was it very doubtfull whether the jorney should proceed; and had not the newes of a gallion of the King of Spaine, which was driven into St. John de Porterico with two millions and a halfe of tresure, come unto them by the reporte of certaine prisoners, whereof they advertised Her Majestie, it is very likely it had been broken; but Her Majestie, persuaded by them of the easie takinge therof, comanded them to haste their departure.

So on Thursday, being the 28th of August, in the year 1595, havinge stayed two moneth in Plimouth, we went thence twenty-seven sail, and were two thousand five hundred men of all sortes. This fleet was devided into two squadrons; not that it was so appointed by Her Majestie, for from her was granted as powerfull authoritie unto eyther of them over the whole as any parte, but Sir Francis victualinge the one halfe and Sir John the other, it made them, as men afectinge what they had done, to chalenge a greater prerogative over them than the whole; wherin they wronged themselves and the action, for wee had not runne sixty or seventy leagues in our course, before a flagge of councell was put out in the Garlande, unto which all commanders with the chiefe masters and gentlemen repayred. Sir Francis complayned that he had a three hundred men more in his squadron then were in the other, and that he was much pestered in his owne shipp, wherof he would gladly be eased. Sir John gave no other hearinge to this motion, but seemed to dislike that he should bring more than was concluded betwixt them, and this drewe them to some chollericke speeches. But Sir John would not receave any unles he were entreated: to this Sir Francis' stout hearte could never be driven. This was on the second of September, and after they were somwhat qualified, they acquainted us that Sir Thomas Baskerville, our coronell generall, was of theyr counsayle by vertue of the broade seale, and that they would take unto them Sir Nicholas Clifforde and the other captains appointed by Her Majestie, who were, eleven for the land, four for the shippes in which they themselves went not. They gave us instructions for directinge our course, if, by foule weather or mischange, any should be severed, and orders what alowances we should put our men into for preservation of victualls, with other necessary instructions. In the end, Sir John revealed the places whither wee were bound, in hearinge of the basest mariner; observinge therin no warlike or provident advice, nor was it ever amended to the time of theyr deaths, but so he named St. John de Porterico, where the treasure before spoken of was to be taken, even withoute blowes, from whence we should go direct to Nombre de Dios, and so over land to Panama. What other things should fall out by the way, he esteemed them not worth the naminge, this being sufficient to make a far greater armie rich to theyr content.

Some seven or eight days after this, we were called aborde the Defiance, where, Sir Francis Drake propoundinge unto us whether we should give upon the Canaries or Maderas (for he was resolved to put for one of them by the way), we seeinge his bent and the earnestnes of the coronel generall, together with the apparent likelihood of profit, might soon have bin drawen therto; but consideringe the weightie matters we had undertaken and how needfull it was to hasten us thether [we did not immediately assent]. But General Hawkins utterly mislikinge this motion, it beinge a matter, as hee saide, never before thought of, [he declared he] knewe no cause why the fleete should staye in any place till they came to the Indies, unles it should be by his takinge in of so greate numbers to consume his waters and other provision; the which, if Sir Francis would acknowledge, hee would ridde him and relieve him the best hee could. Now the fyer which laye hid in theyr stomacks began to breake forth, and had not the coronell pacified them, it would have growen farther; but theyr heat somwhat abated, and they concluded to dine next day aboarde the Garlande with Sir John, when it was resolved that we should put for the Grand Canaries, though, in my conscience, whatsoever his tonge saide, Sir John's harte was againste.

These matters were well qualified, and for that place we shaped our course, in which we met with a small flemminge bounde for the Streights and a small manne of warre of Waymouth, who kept us companie to the Canaries. On Wensday, the twenty-fourth day, we had sight of Lancerotta and Forteventura. The twenty-fifth at night we descried the Canaries, it beinge a monthe after our departure from Plymouth. On Friday, beinge the twenty-sixth, we came to anchor, some saker shott from a forte which stands to the west norwest of the harboure. Sir Francis spent much time in seekinge out the fittest place to land; the enemie therby gaininge time to drawe theyr forces in rediness to impeach our approach. At length we puttinge for the shore in our boats and pinnaces, found a great seege and such power of men to encounter us, that it was then thought it would hazarde the whole action if we should give further upon it, wherupon we returned without recevinge or doinge any harme worthy the writinge; but, undoubtedly, had we lanced under the forte at our first cominge to anchor, wee had put fayre to bee possessors of the towne, for the delayes gave the enemie greate stomackes and daunted our owne; and it beinge the first service our new men were brought into, it was to be doubted they would prove the worse the whole jorney followinge.

We presently wayed hence and came to anchor the twenty-seventh at the west south west part of this islande, where wee watered. Here Captaine Grimstone, one of the twelve captaines for lande, was slaine by the mountainors, with his boy and a surgeon. Hence wee departed the twenty-eighth, houldinge our course south-west three weeks, then we ran west south west and west and by south till the twenty-seventh of October, on which day we had sight of Maten, an island lying south-est from Dominica. Our generalls ment to water at Guadalupe, for Dominica beinge inhabited by Indians, our men straglinge soon would have their throates cutte. Generall Drake lyinge ahead the fleet, ran in by the mouth of Dominica, Sir John by south. The twenty-ninth we anchored under Guadalupe; Sir Francis beinge there a daye before us. On the thirtieth, Josias, captaine of the Delight, brought newes to the generalls, that the Francis, a small shippe of companie, was taken by nine frigotts, wherupon Sir Francis would presently have folowed them either with the whole fleete or some parte, for that he knew our intentions were discovered by reason they were so openly made knowne, as I afore have set downe, by Sir John Hawkins. Sir John would in no wise agree to eyther of these motions, and he was assisted in his opinion by Sir Nicholas Clifforde, all others furtheringe his desires, which might be a means to staye them for goinge into Porterico before us; but Sir John prevayled, for that hee was sickly, Sir Francis beinge loth to breed his further disquiet. The reason of his stay was, to trimme his shippes, mounte his ordinance, take in water, set by some new pinnaces, and to make things in that rediness, that he cared not to meet with the king's whole fleete. Heere we stayed doinge these necessaries three dayes. This is a desarte, and was without inhabitants.

On the fourth of November we departed, and being becalmed under the lee of the land, Sir Francis caused the Richarde, one of the victuallers, to be unladen and sunk. The eighth wee anchored amonge the Virginees, other west ilandes: heere we drew our companie on shore, that every man might knowe his colours, and wee founde our companie shorte of the one thousand two hundred promised for lande service, few of the captains having above ninety, most not eighty, some not fifty; which fell out partly for that the generalls had selected to them a companie for theyr guarde, of many of the gallantest men of the army. Sir John his sicknes incresed. Sir Francis apointed captaines to the merchants' shippes: this consumed time till the eleventh, when we passed a sounde, though, by our mariners, never passed by fleet afore, and we came to anchor before Porterico on the twelfth, about three of the clocke in the afternoone, at what time Sir John Hawkins died. I made my men ready presently to have landed, knowinge that our sodaine resolution would greatly have danted the enemie, and have held our [own men] in opinion of assured victory; but I was countermanded by authoritie, and during the time of our deliberation, the enemie labored by all meanes to cause us to disankar, so workinge, that within an houre hee had planted three or four pieces of artillery upon the shore next unto us, and playinge upon the Defiance, knowing her to be the Admirall, whilest our generalls sate at souper with Sir Nicholas Clifford and diverse other, a shotte came amongst them, wherwith Sir Nicholas, Brute, Brown, Captain Strafford, who had Greenstone's company, and some standers by, were hurte. Sir Nicholas died that night, so secondinge Sir John Hawkins in his death as he did in his opinion at Guadalupe. My brother Browne lived five or six days after, and died much bewayled. This shotte made our generall to way and fall further to the westward, where we rode safely. The five frigotts before spoken of rode within their forts: wee had no place nowe to lande our men but within them in the face of the towne, which was dangerous, for that both shippes and forts could playe on us; it was therefore concluded that boats should fire them where they rode. Captain Poore and mysealfe had the comande of this service; for the regiments, Captain Salisburie comandinge; the grand captain companye was sent by the generalls; diverse sea commanders were also sent; and on the thirteenth at night passinge in harde under the forte, we set three of them on fire; only one of which, it was my chance to undertake, was burnt; on the others, the fire held not by reason that being once out they were not maintained with newe. The burnte shippe gave a greate light, the enemie thereby playinge upon us with their ordinance and small shotte as if it had been fayre daye, and sinkinge some of our boates: a man could hardly comande his mariners to row, they foolishly thinkinge every place more dangerous than where they were, when, indeede, none was sure. Thus doinge no harme, we returned with two or three prisoners, when, indeede, in my poore oppinion, it had binne an easier matter to bringe them out of the harborowe than fire them as wee did, for our men aboard the shippes numbred five thousand one hundred and sixty peeces of artillerie that played on us during this service; and it had binne less dangerous to have abidden them close in the frigotts and in the darke than as wee did; but great comanders many tymes fayle in theyre judgment, beinge crost by a compartner; but I had cause of more griefe than the Indies could yielde mee of joye, losinge my Alfierez,[2] Davis Pursell; Mr. Vaughan, a brother-in-law of Sir John Hawkins, with three others; Thomas Powton, with five or six more hurte and maimed; and was somwhat discomfited, for the generall feigned heere to set up his rest; but examininge the prisoners, by whom hee understoode that these frigotts were sent for his treasure, and that they would have fallen amonge us at Guadalupe had they not taken the Francis, his minde altered: callinge to counsaile, he comanded us to give our opinions what we thought of the strength of the place. Most thought it would hazard the whole action. But one Rush, a captaine, more to mee aleadged that without better puttinge for it, [than by] the bare lookinge upon the outside of the

[2] Ensign (borrowed from the Arabic).

forts, we could hardly give such judgment; and I set it playnely under my hande, that if we resolutely attempted it, all was ours ; and that I persuaded mysealfe no towne in the Indies could yielde us more honnor or profitte. The generall presently saide: "I will bring thee to twenty places farre more wealthye and easier to be gotten." Such-like speeches I thinke had bewitched the coronell, for he most desired him to hasten him hence.

The enemie, the day after we had fired the frigotts, suncke together four to save us labour, but chiefly to strengthen their fortes: two other greate shippes they suncke and fired in the mouth of the harborowe to give them light to playe on us from theyr fortes as we entred the first night. And hence we went the fifteenth. Heere I left all hope of good successe.

On the nineteenth we came to anchor in a fayre baye (the baye of Sta. Jermana), at the westermost part of the ilande, where wee stayed till the twenty-fourth, settinge up more newe pinnaces and unlodinge the other newe victualler, the generall takinge the most parte into his owne shippe as he did of the former. Captaine Yorke, in the Hope, was made vice-admirall. This is a very pleasant and fertile ilande, having upon it goode store of cattell, fruites, and fish, with all thinges necessary to man's sustenance; and were it well manured, no place could yielde it in greater abundance or better. Departing hence, we had our course for Corasaw.[3] The seconde daye after our puttinge of, the Exchange, a small shippe, spronge her mast, and was sunke; the men and parte of the victualls were saved by other shippes. Twenty-ninth.—Upon Corasaw there is great store of cattell and goates, and we fell with it upon Saturday the twenty-ninth; but our generall, deceaved by the currante and westerly course, made it for Arabir,[4] an iland lyinge ten or twelve leagues to the westwarde, and so made no staye, when, next morninge descryenge whether hee founde his error, wee bore with Cape De la Vela, and

[3] Curaçoa. [4] Aruba.

from thence our coronell, with all the companies in the pinnaces and boates were sent to the cittie of Rio de la Hacha, and with small resistance wee tooke it the first of December at night. The generall came unto us the next morning with the fleete. This towne was left bare of goodes: the inhabitants havinge intelligence of our cominge, had caried all in the woodes, and hid theyr treasure in casshes;[5] but, stayinge heere seventeen days, wee made so goode search, that little remained unfounde within four leagues of the towne. We tooke many prisoners, Spaniards and negroes, some slaves repairinge to us voluntarily. The generall with two hundred men went in boates to Lancheria, which is a place where they fish for pearle, standinge ten leagues to the estwarde of theyr towne, from whence they brought goode store of pearle, and tooke a carvell, in which was some monie, wine, and myrr.

During our stay heere, the governor once, diverse others often, repaired unto us to redeeme theyr towne, Lancheria, boates and slaves. They did this to gaine time to convey away the kinge's treasure and to advertyse theyr neighbour towne to convey their treasure in more safetye then themselves had done; for the whole (except the slaves who voluntarily repayred unto us) was yielded unto them for twenty-four thousand peasos, five shillings and sixpence a peece, to bee payde in pearles; bringinge these to theyr towne at the daye and valuinge in double the price they were worth. Our generall delivered the hostages and set their towne (Lancheria) and boates on fire, carryinge their slaves with us. The wealth we had heere was given to countervayle the charge of the jorney; but I feare it will not so prove in the end. Our vice-admirall, Captaine Yorcke, died heere of sicknes. This is an exceedinge goode countrye, champion and well inhabited; great store of cattayle, horses, sheepe, goates, fish, and fowle, wheron wee fedde, but smale

[5] The French *caches*, hiding places.

store of graine or fruite neere the towne, rich only in pearle and cattell.

The twentieth, being Saturday, we came to St. Tomarta.[6] We suncke two catches before we came to Rio de la Hacha, which we brought out of England. Presently, upon our coming to anchors, we landed and gave upon the town. We found small resistance more than a fewe shotte playinge out of the woodes as we marched towards the towne. Companies were presently sent abroade to discover and searche the countrye. The inhabitants had to long forewarninge to carry theyr goods out of our possibilitie to find them in so short time; little or nothing of valew was gotten, only the Leiftenant-governor and some others were taken prisoners; and firyinge the towne the twenty-first, we departed.

Captain Worrell, our trenchmaster, died at this towne of sicknes. This was a very prettie towne, and six leagues off there was a gould mine. If part of our companie had been sent thither upon our first arrival at Rio de la Hacha, doubtles we had done much goode, but now they had scrube it very bare. In this place was great store of fruite and much fernandobuck;[7] for that the winde blewe so extremely, and the rode wilde, we could not shippe it. Before we departed hence, it was concluded that we should passe Cartagena and go directly for Nombre de Dios. We anchored in the rode on Sunday followinge, beinge the twenty-seventh; and landinge presently, receavinge some small shotte from the towne, we founde small resistance more than a little forte at the east side of theyr towne, in which they had left one peece of ordinance which brake at the first shotte. They gave upon us as we gave upon them: certaine prisoners were taken in the flyinge, who made it knowne, that havinge intelligence, longe before, of our cominge, theyr treasure was

6 Sta. Martha.

7 Brasil wood, the produce of Pernambuco, or, as the name was originally written, Fernandobuco.

conveyed to places of more safetie, eyther to Panama or secretly hidden; and it might very well bee, for the towne was left very bare; wherefore it was resolved that we should hasten with speed for Panama. Nombre de Dios standeth on the north-side sea, Panama upon the south, distant some eighteen or nineteen leagues. There were only two wayes to get thither; one by the river Chagree, which lyeth to the westward twenty leagues; upon this it is passable within five leagues of Panama: the other through deserts and over mountaines voide of inhabitants: this was troublesom and harde, as well for want of means to carry our provision of meate and munition as for the ill passage with an armie through these deserts and unknown places. That by the river our generall held more dangerous, fayninge there was no place for our fleet to wade safely. This made our coronell to yeelde to the waye by the mountaine, though he and others foresawe the danger before our settinge hence; but he resolved to make tryall of what coulde be done.

So on Monday the twenty-ninth we began our jorney, takinge with us the strongest and lustiest of our armie, to the number of fifty men and seven colours. Before our settinge hence, we buried Captaine Arnolde Baskerville, our serjant-major generall, a gallant gentleman. The first daye we marched three leagues; the next, six leagues, where we came to a greate house which the enemie had sett on fire, it beinge a place where the kinge's mules do use to lodge cominge from Panama to Nombre de Dios with his treasure: it is the mid-way betwixt both places. The house would receave five hundred horses. We had not marched fully a league on Wednesday morninge, when we came to a place fortified upon the toppe of an hill, which the enemie defended. We had noe other way to passe nor noe means to make our approach but a very deepe lande, where but one could passe at once, unles it were by clammeringe upon the bancks and creepinge up the hill through the brakes, which some of our men did, and came to the trees which they had plasshed to make theyr palizadoe, over which they coulde not passe, the many bowes so hindered them. It was my chance, clammeringe up the banckes to repaire to three musketters which I had holpen up, to fall directly betwixt two of theyr places fortified, cominge unto two paths by which they fetched their water, and givinge presently upon them, the place being open, my small number found to goode resistance, and I was driven to retire with the losse of these fewe. Heere was the only place to beate them from theyr houlde, wherof I sent the coronell worde, Captaine Poore and Bartlett and others repayringe to me. I shewed them the path; we heard the enemie plasshinge and fellinge of trees farre before us. The coronell sent for us to come unto him: he debated with us what he foresaw before our cominge from Nombre de Dios, and though he thought, in his oppinion, we should feare the enemie hence, yet, havinge retreits upon retreits, they would kill our best men without takinge little or any hurte themselves; and our men began to drop apace; our powder and match were spoilde by much rain and waters which we had passed, unles it were such as som of our souldiers had with more care preserved. The provision for meate at our coming from Nombre de Dios was seven or eight cakes of bisked or ruske for a man, which was eyther by wette spoyled, or theyr greediness had devoured; so there remained to fewe one daye's bread; to most none at all. Our hurte men, as Captaine Nicholas Baskerville and some other of accounte, we should be driven to leave to the mercie of the enemie, unles they could houlde companie. Before our cominge to Panama, had we beaten them from all these houlds, which I think would have bin to dangerous for us to have attempted, consideringe the estate we were in, we must have fought with them at a bridge where they had intrenched themselves in a far greater number than we were; and it is manifest, if we had not within three days gotten some releife, we had bin overthrowen, though no enemie had fought against us. But our stomacks callinge these, with other dangers, to his carefull consideration, he resolved to retire, and so commanded us to cause the slaine to be throwne out of sight, the hurte to be sent to the quarter from whence we came that morninge, and the rest to be drawen away. Heere were slaine Captaine Marchant, our quarter-master, with some other officers, gentlemen, and souldiers. Upon our coming to the quarter, the coronell took view of the hurte, and for such as could ride he procured all the horses of the armie; for the other, he entreated the enemie to entreate them kindly, as they expected the like from us towards theyrs, of which we had a farre greater number.

On the seconde of January we returned to Nombre de Dios; our men so wearied with the ilnes of the waye, surbaited for want of shoes, and weake with theyr diet, that it would have bin a poor dayes service that we should have done upon an enimie had they been there to resist us. I am persuaded that never armie, great or small, undertooke a march through to unknown places so weakly provided and with so small means to help themselves, unles it might be some few goinge covertly to do som sodaine exploite before it were thought of by the enemie, and so returne unspied; for, undoubtedly, two hundred men foreknowinge their intentions and provided with all things necessarie, are able to breake or weaken the greatest force that any prince in Christendome can bringe thither, if he had place to finde more than we had. This marche had made many swere that he will never venture to buy gould at such a price againe. I confesse noble spiritts, desirous to do service to theyr prince and country, may soon be persuaded to all hardnes and danger; but havinge once made tryall therof, would be very loth, as I suppose, to carry any force that way againe; for beholdinge it in many places, a man would judge it dangerous for one man to passe alone, almost impossible for horses and an armie.

The daye that our generall had newes of our returne, he ment to way and fall nearer to the river Chagree with the fleete, leavinge some few to bringe us if we were enforced to retire, wherof hee little doubted. But beinge beaten from the place where it appeered all his hopes rested for gayninge to himselfe and others this masse of treasure which he so confidently promised before, it was high time for him to devise of some other course. Wherfore, on the fourth of January, he called us to counsayle, and debated with us what was nowe to be done. All these parties had notice long before of all our intentions, as it appeered by letters written from the governor of Lima to the governor of Panama and Numbre de Dios, givinge them advice to be carefull and to looke well to themselves, for that Drake and Hawkins were makinge readie in England to come upon them. Lima is distant from these places more than three hundred leagues, all overlayed with snakes. It appeareth that they had good intelligence. This made them to convey theyr treasure to places which they resolved to defend with better force than we were able to attempt. Like as upon the cominge of the sun, dewes and mistes begin to vanish, so our blinded eyes began now to open, and wee founde that the glorious speeches, of an hundred places that they knew in the Indies to make us rich, was but a baite to drawe Her Majestie to give them honorable employments and us to adventure our lives for theyr glory; for now cards and mappes must bee our cheefest directors, hee beinge in these partes at the furthest limit of his knowledge. There hee found out a place called Laguna de Nichoragua, upon which standeth certaine townes, as Granada, Leon, and others; also the bay of Honduras, a place knowne to be of small wealth by itsealfe, unles it be brought thither to be imbarqued for Spaine. He demanded which of those we would attempt; our coronell saide, bothe, one after another, and all to little to content us if wee tooke them. It was then resolved that we should first for the river, and as matters fell out, for the other. Numbre de Dios, together with their negroe towne were fyred; and we suncke and fyred fourteen small frigotts which we founde in the rode. We gott here twenty barres of silver, with som gould and certaine plate; more would have benne founde, had it bene well sought; but our generall thought it folly to gather our harvest graine by graine, beinge so likely at Panama to thrust our handes into the whole heapes: and after our returne, beinge troubled in minde, hee seemed little to regard any consayle that should be given him to that purpose, but to hasten thence as fast as he might. This is a most wealthy place, being setled upon a grounde full of camphyre, environed with hilly woodes and mountaines, the bottom a dampish fen. Hence wee departed the fifth, and held our course for Nichragua.

On the ninth we founde a very deepe and dangerous baye, playinge it here up and downe: all men weary of the place. The tenth we descried a small iland called Escudes, where we came to anchor: and here we tooke a frygotte which was an advice of the kinge's. By this we learned that the townes standinge upon this lake, were of small wealth and very dangerous, by reason of many shoals and greate roughes our mariners should have, it beinge an hundred leagues: yet if the winde would have permitted, we had assuredly put for them, and never returned to one halfe againe. Heere we stayed, at a waste island where there was no reliefe but a few tortoyses for such as could catch them, twelve days. This is counted the sickliest place of the Indies; and heere died many of our men, victualls beginninge to growe scarse with us. In the end, findinge the winde to continue contrary, he resolved to departe, and to take the winde as God sent it.

So on the twenty-second we went hence, having there buried Captaine Plott, Egerton, and divers others. I questioned with our generall, beinge often private with him whilst we stayed heere, to see whether hee would reveale unto mee any of his purposes; and I demanded of him, why hee so often conjured me, beinge in England, to stay with him in these partes as longe as himselfe, and where the place was. He answered me with griefe, protestinge that hee was as ignorant of the Indies as mysealfe, and that he never thought any place could be so changed, as it were from a delitious and pleasant arbour into a wast and desarte wildernesse; besides the variableness of the winde and weather, so stormie and blusterous as hee never sawe it before. But hee most wondred that since his cominge out of England he never sawe sayle worth givinge chace unto: yet in the greatness of his minde, hee would, in the end, conclude with these wordes: "It matters not, man; God hath many thinges in store for us; and I knowe many means to do Her Majestie good service and to make us riche, for we must have gould before wee see Englande"; when, goode gentleman, (in my conceite) it fared with him as with some careles livinge man who prodigally consumes his time, fondly perswadinge himselfe that the nurse that fedde him in his childhood will likewise nourish him in his ould age, and, finding the dugge dried and withered, enforced then to behould his folly, tormented in mind, dieth with a starved bodie. Hee had, beside his own adventure, gaged his owne reputation greatly, in promisinge Her Majestie to do her honorable service, and to returne her a very profitable adventure; and havinge sufficiently experienced, for seven or eight years together, how hard it was to regain favour once ill thought of, the mistresse of his fortune now leavinge him to yield to a discontented minde. And since our returne from Panama he never caried mirth nor joy in his face; yet no man hee loved must conjecture that hee tooke thought thereof. But heere hee began to grow sickly. At this iland we suncke a carvell which we brought out of England, puttinge her men and victualls into a last taken frigott. From hence a great currante setts towards the estward; by reason wherof, with the scant of winde we had on Wednesday, beinge the twenty-eight, we came to Portabella, which is within eight or nine leagues of Numbre de Dios. It was the best harborough we came unto sence we left Plymouth.

This morninge, about seven of the clocke, Sir Francis died. The next day Sir Thomas Baskerville caried him a league of, and buried him in the sea. In this place, the inhabitants of Numbre de Dios meant to build a towne, it beinge far more healthye than where they dwell. Heere they began a forte which alreadie cost the kinge seven thousand purses, and a fewe houses towards their town, which they called Civitas Sti. Philippi. Them we fired, rasinge the fortification to the grounde. Heere we found, as in other places, all abandoned; theyr ordinance cast into the sea, some of which we founde, and caried aboard the Garland.

Our generalls beinge dead, most men's heartes were bent to hasten for England as soon as they might; but Sir Thomas Baskervile havinge the comand of the armie by vertue of Her Majestie's broad seale, endeavoured to prevent the disseveringe of the fleet, and to that end, talked with such as hee hearde intended to quite companie before they were disembogued, and drew all companies to subscribe to certaine articles signifyinge our purposes—viz., that puttinge hence, wee should turne it backe to St. Tomarto[8] if the winde would suffer us, otherwise to run over for Jamaica, where it was thought we should bee refreshed with some victualls. Matters thus concluded, the Delight, the Elizabeth, and our late taken frigotts were suncke. Many of the negro men and base prisoners were here put on shore; and heere we wayed on Sunday the eighth of February. Our victualls began to shorten apace, yet we had lyen a longe time at very harde alowance,—four men each morninge one quarte of beere and cake of biskett for diner, and for supper one quarte of beere

[8] Santa Martha.

and two cakes of biskett and two cans of water, with a pinte of pease or half a pinte of rise or somwhat more of oatemeale. This was our allowance beinge at Portabella and six weekes before, but that we had sometime stockfish. From thence there is a current that sets to the eastward, by the helpe of which, on the fourteenth, wee had sight of an iland shorte of Carthagena fifteen or sixteen leagues; further than this wee could not go to the estward, for that the current had left us. The fifteenth at night, it beinge faire weather, we lost sight of our fleete. Heere as I grew discontented, knowinge it touched my poore regulation so to leave the armie; and I had many thinges to perswade mee that it was done of purpose by the captaine and master, therby gaininge an excuse to departe; I shewed the captaine of the danger he should run into by leavinge so honorable forces when they had neede of our companie: and God knoweth that had I had but judgment which way to have cast for them, I would rather have lost my life then so forsake the like. He deposed on the bible, and Christianitie made me believe him. But playinge it up and downe about twelve of the clocke, and discoveringe none of them, the wind blew so contrary that the seamen affirmed by houldinge this course we should be cast backe in the bay, and they perswaded that our fleete could not attaine St. Tomarto, but were gone over for Jamaica, whither they would follow then. I plainly forsaw that if we missed them there, it was like that we should no more meete till we came to England, which would have made me to perswade a longer search upon the maine; but my hope of their beinge there, together with the weakness of our men and the small meanes we had to retaine them, fearinge lest my delay might endanger Her Majesties shippes and the whole companie, I yielded to theyr perswasions. We were in ten degrees and a halfe when we put from hence, and we came till the twenty-second, when we had sight of a very dangerous shoale which our seamen thought they had passed neare two dayes before. If we had fallen with it in the night we had bin all lost. The shoale is named Secrana.

On Shrove Wensday, being the twenty-fourth, we fell with Jamaica, and by meanes of a Mulatow and an Indian, we had, this night, forty bundles of dried beife, which served our whole companie so many dayes. We came to anchor at the westermost parte of the iland, in a faire, sandie bay, where we watered, and stayed, in hope to have some newes of our fleete, seven dayes. This, our stay, brought no intelligence, wherfore our seamen thought that our fleet, not able to recover this place, were fallen eyther with Cape Corantes or Cape St. Antoine[9]; these places we ment to touch in our course; and hence we went the first of March. On the sixth we sawe a shippe on the leaward of us, and the next morninge we made her to be the Pegasine, one of our fleete, who, as they sayde, lost the admirall neere the time as we did, beinge by the coronell sent to the Susan Bonaventure, whom they left in greate distresse, by reason of a lake they had taken, and I greatly feared, by theyr reporte, they are perished. There were in her one hundred and thirty or one hundred and forty persons, many gallant gentlemen and good men. If they perish, this shippe shall repent it. Houldinge our course for these places, we descried five sayles a stern of us. We stayed for them, and soone made them to be none of our fleete; and we had good reason to perswade us they were enimies. They had the winde of us, but we soone regained it upon them, which made them, upon a peece of ordinance shott of by the greatest shippe, tacke about; we tackt with them; when the captain of this shippe faithfully protested unto me not to shoote a peece of ordinance till we came boord and boorde, and then I promised him, with our small shot, to win the greatest or lose our persons. This we might have done without endanger-

[9] C. Corrientes and C. St. Antonio, at the western extremity of Cuba.

inge Her Majestie's shippes; but our enimie, playinge upon us with theyr ordinance, made our gunners fall to it ere we were at musket shot, and no nearer could I bringe them, though I had no hope to take any of them but by boordinge. Heere we popt away powder and shott to no purpose, for most of our gunners would hardly have stricken Paule's steeple had it stoode there. I am a yonge seaman, yet my small judgment and knowledge makes me avowe, that never shippe of Her Majestie's went so vilely manned out of her kingdom; not twenty of them worthy to come into her shippes; and I know not what had possessed the captaine, but his mind was cleane altered, tellinge me that he had no authoritie to lay any shippe aboorde, wherby he might endanger this, Her Majestie's; and they beinge, as he sayd, the kinge's men of warre, they would rather fire with us than be taken. Had I beene a marchant of her burden (God favoringe me), they would have bin mine, as many as stoode to the tryall of theyr fortune; but the paltrie Pegosie we lately met withall never came neere us by a league, which was some colour to our men to give them over. So after I had endeavored by mysealfe, my lewetenant and other gentlemen, by perswasion, to worke the captaine resolutely to attempt them, and findinge no disposition in him but to consume powder and shott to no purpose, but firinge it in the ayer, I yielded to give them over, perswadinge mysealfe that God had even ordained that we should not with any nature attempt where we were resisted with never so weake forces. Thus away we went, and the winde choppinge us southerly, our seamen held that our fleete coulde neither ride at Corants nor at St. Antony, which made me condescend to leave the Indies, with all her treasure, and to plye the next course to disembogue,[10] for little hope was left me that we should do Her Majestie any service, or good to our selves, when, upon the

[10] *Disembogue* signifies here (as in p. 20, l. 22), to pass the *Bocas*; to get clear of the narrow seas and enter the ocean.

feigned excuses of endangering her shippes which she sent orth to fight if occasion were offered; and to perswade my-sealfe that Her Majestie priseth not her ships deerer than the lives of so many faithful subjects, who gladly would have ventured theyr lives, and upon no brain-sick humour, but from a trew desire to do Her Highness some service for the charge and adventure she had been at in this glorious spoken-of jorney. Fortune's child was dead, thinges would not fall into our mouthes, nor riches be our portions, howe dearly soever we adventured for them. Thus avoydinge Silla (after the proverbe), we felle into Charibdis, and indeede we were not nowe farre from it.

Our master, a careful ould man, but not experienced upon these coastes, rather followinge the advice of others than reliengе on his owne judgment, brought us, on the twelfth, three hours before daye, into a very shallow water, upon a dangerous bancke, which some held to be the Meltilettes, others for the Tortugas, eyther like enough to have swallowed us, had not God blest us with fayre weather. Freinge ourselves of this danger, upon Monday the fifteenth of March we entered the gulfe, and by ten of the clocke we brought the Cape of Florida west of us. On the seventeenth (the Lord be thanked) we were disembogued. After this, we ran with most fowle weather and contrary windes till the first of May, when we had soundinge in ninety fathoms, beinge in the Channell, and on the third we had sight of Sylly; the which day, ere night, we came to anchor, (the Lord be therefore praysed) 1596.

To give mine oppinion of the Indies, I verily think that filchinge men of warre shall do more goode then such a fleete, if they have aine forewarninge of theyr cominge. And unles Her Majestie will undertake so royally as to dispossesse him of the landes of Porterico, Hispaniola, and Cuba, her charge will be greater in sendinge thither, then the profitt such a fleet can returne, for havinge but a fewe days warninge, it is easy for them to convey theyr goods into assured safetie, as experience hath taught us. Theyr townes they dare not redeeme, beinge enjoyned the contrary by the kinge's comandment. These places will be taken and possessed by two thousand men; and by this Her Majestie might debarre the kinge of Spain of his whole profitt of the Indies: and the first gaininge them will return her a sufficient requittal for her adventure. God grant I may live to see such an enterprise put in practise; and the kinge of Spaine will speedily flye to what conditions of peace Her Majestie will require.

Thus I have truly set down the whole discourse of our voyage, usinge therin many idle wordes and ill-compared sentences. It was done on the sea, which I thinke can alter any disposition. Your loves, I thinke, can pardon these faltes, and secret them from the vewe of others.

The first of March the fleete fell with the Pinnas,[11] on the land of Cuba, which day they had sight of the Spanish fleete by eleven of the clocke; where Sir Thomas Baskervile gave directions for the fleete as thus:—the Garland, being admirall, with one halfe of the fleete to have the vanguard; the Hope, beinge vice-admirall, with the other halfe, the rereward. The fight continued fiercely three hours within muskett shott. That night they saw the Spanish Vice-admirall, a ship of seven hundred tonne, burned, with other six lost and suncke by the next morninge, when they departed. The Hope received a leake and was forced to go from the fleete to an iland, called St. Crusado, inhabited by canniballs, where they had store of hens and Indian wheate for nine weekes. March eighth, the fleete shott the gulfe and came for England, leavinge Florida on the starboard side; and when they came to the Inchanted Islands they were dispersed, and came home one by one.

THOMAS MAYNARDE.

[11] The Isla de Pinos.

RELACION

DE LO SUCEDIDO

EN SAN JUAN DE PUERTO RICO DE LAS YNDIAS,

CON LA ARMADA YNGLESA

DEL CARGO DE

FRANCIS DRAQUE Y JUAN AQUINES,

A LOS 23RD DE NOVIEMBRE DE

1595.

RELACION DE LO SUCEDIDO, ETC.

AVIENDO salido de la Avana para Espana el general Sancho Pardo y Osorio a los 10 de Março deste año, con la capitana de la flota de tierra firme de su cargo, en conserva de la armada de don Fran°. Coloma, y aviendose allado[1] en la tormenta que corrio desembocada de la canal a los 15 del dho mes en altura de 28 grados y medio, sin arbol mayor, rompido el timon, y la nao haciendo mucha agua, apartada de las demas, imposibilitada de seguir su viage, para salvar las vidas de 300 personas que en ella venian y dos millones de oro y plata de su Magestad y particulares, con acuerdo y parecer del vehedor Martin Vomero de Caamaño y de los pilotos y demas personas platicas que alli se allaron, aribo a Puerto rico a donde bien milagrosamente llego a los 9 de April, y alli desembarco y puso la Plata en la fortaleça de la ciudad. Luego el dho general despacho a su Magestad primero y secundo aviso haciendoles saver su ariba, para que mandase lo que hubiese de haçer, y parece que la divina [providencia] permitio por secretos suyos que la orden, pudiendo ser antes, llegare a tiempo que no solo aseguro la Plata sino esta tierra y seria posible todas las Yndias, por lo que adelante se vera, aquien se pueden dar muchas gratias.

Pocos dias despues de aver despachado los dhos avisos, los tuvo de su Magestad el governador desta ysla Pedro Suares

[1] For hallado, as *Avana* (above) for Havana, *an* (lower down) for han, *avito* for habito, &c.

Coronel en que le aviso en que en Yngalaterra se aprestava una gruesa armada para venir aganar esta ysla en tiempo de embierno, por pareçer que entonçes estaria menos apercevida. Entendidos por el general y el dho veedor los dhos avisos se juntaron con el governador y con Fran°. Cid, capitan de la ynfanteria deste presidio, y tratado y conferido las preventiones que se debian haçer para seguridad de la tierra y Plata de su Magestad para que en caso que el enemigo viniese no se apoderase de todo ello, fueron todos juntos a reconecer los sitios y baraderos por donde el enemigo podia acometer y echar gente en tierra, y que en las partes que al general le parecio, mando plantar parte de la artilleria de su capitana y atravesar la nao en la canal del puerto, para que quando viniese el enemigo, se echase a fondo y sele çegase la entrada, pareciendo que por alli avia de acometer y lo demas riesgo, y contener la gente en buena guarida; se estubo en espera de la orden de su Magestad para hacer su viage.

A los 13th de Nobiembre deste año llego a este puerto Don Pedro Tello de Guzman, con las cincas fragatas de su Magestad para que el general Sancho Pardo embarcase en ella la plata de su Magestad y se fuese la buelta de españa, haciendo officio de su Almirante el dho Pedro Tello, el qual despues de aver entregado sus despachos, le dijo al dho general como viniendo en seguimiento de su viage, avian encontrado dos navios yngleses en la ysla de Guadalupe, que se avian apartado de la armada ynglesa y que su almirante Gonçalo Mendez de Canço avia rendido y echado a fondo el uno, despues de aver le sacado os yngleses prisiones y que yendo el dho Don Pedro en seguimiento del otro navio descubrio nueve velas de la armada del enemigo, y desque las vio viro la otra buelta siguiendo su viage; y que los dhos yngleses prisioneros avian declarado que cerca de alli en la misma ysla de Guadalupe a la banda del sur, estava surta la armada de la reyna de yngalaterra, y aprestando lanchas con veinte y cinco navios, los seis de los galeones de la reyna de 800 toneladas y otros dos del mesmo porte de particulares, y todos en dos esquadras, y por generales Fran°. Draque y Juan Aquines, governando la derota y cosas de tierra Fran°. Draque y su lugarteniente en tierra Don Thomas Vasquezarfil; y que traia la armada 30[2] infantes y 10,500 marineros bien artillados, y que venian derechos a Puerto rico, como parecia por la ynstruccion que se le tomo al capitan del dho navio yngles en la qual se le ordeno en caso que por alguno forçoso se apartase, viniese a Puerto rico, donde le aguardarian 10 dias, y que alli se dexarian orden adonde avian de yr despues, sin declarar otro disegno; y que conforme a esto el dho Don Pedro venia temeroso que no ubiese venido delante y estubiese ganada la tierra, y que puesto no avia sido, tenia por cierto que aes otro dia estaria sobre el puerto, y que conforme a esto el general ordenase su partida como mas pareciese combenir.

Visto el general Sancho Pardo la relacion del dho Don Pedro Tello y su Almirante Gonçalo Mendez y que esta nueba le allava en la cama y indispuesto de enfermidad, de algunos dias avia estava con ella, hiço avisar a Obispo y al governador, pidiendoles se viesen con el y los capitanes de fragatas Marco Antonio Becerra, cabo de la compania de Arcabuçeros, y Pedro de Guia del avito de San Juan, y Domingo de Ynsaurraga, Fran°. Gomez, capitan deste presidio, y el veedor Martin Vomero de Caamaño, Juan de la Vera, contador de las fragatas; y todos juntos en su posada y aviendo tratado y propuesto el dho general la relacion que tenia del enemigo y los medios mas combenientes que avia por la seguridad de la tierra y plata; supuesto que la armada enemiga era tanta y esperarse tan breve, y que las fragatas precisamente tenian necesidad de adereçarse y meter agua y leña y embarcarse la plata en que se avian de detener ocho dias por lo menos, y considerando que el enemigo quando estuviese con esta ocupacion, y quando no por el aviso que le

[2] This ought, probably, to be 3000.

pudo dar el otro navio que se vio, que estas fragatas venian por la plata que ya savia que estava aqui, la podia esperar al paso, oque de la tierra se podia apoderar y fortificarse en ella para conquistar a todas las Yndias, en que a su Magestad leseguia gran perjucio y daño de su reputacion.

Todos de unanime conformes acordaron que la tierra se fortificase con la artilleria y gente, y que la nao capitana de tierra firme y otro de Pedro Milanes se echasen a fondo en la canal del puerto para çegar la entrada, y que la plata no se mudase de la fortaleça asta ver como las cosas se ponian, pareciendo estara alli mas segura y en parte donde quando per nuestros pecados se lo ordenava, se pudiera echar al a mar paraque no la goçase el enemigo, y con esta resolucion sean ydo poniendo en execution con mucha priesa y diligencia de noche y de dia todas prevençiones posibles.

El general Sancho Pardo como persona de tanta experientia y que tenia visto y reconoçido los sitios y puertos de la tierra, aseguro al dho Don Pedro Tello y a los que con el venian, que era caso ymposible perderse la tierra quiriendo los nuestros pelear y haçer el deber, y que solo avia tener cuidado del puerto, que la armada no se metiese de golpe, y que par eso era bien se echasen a fondo las dos naos que estava acordado, y en sus espaldas las fragatas con las proas a la mar par resistir la entrada, y que con eso estava segura la tierra y plata de su Magestad, de que seria muy servido, en cuyo nombre les pedio acudiesen a sus obligaciones; y para esto Don Pedro Tello tomo a su cargo la defensa del puerto.

El Obispo offreçio de deçir el otro dia una misa y una platica ala gente, como lo hiço, christianamente encargandole el serviçio de Dios y de su rey, y siempre continuo este officio de noche y de dia visitando los puestos donde la gente estava, puniendo en cada uno un saçerdote y animandolos con mucho exfuerço.

Este dia el governador y general despacharon un barco con aviso a sancto Domingo para que se pusiesen y estubiesen a la mira por si el enemigo yba alla como se entiende y se le escrivio al Presidente, que luego avisase lo mismo a Cartagena y a Sancta Maria.

Luego se hiço muestra de toda la gente de la tierra, y parte de la que avia en las fragatas se desembarco por ser necesario para la tierra; allose en todo a 10,300 personas y en estos 700 de pelea y los 800 de fragatas y capitana de tierra firme, y las demas del presidio y forasteros, en los quales avia 50 de a cavallo con lança y adarga, que todo se repartieron en la forma siguiente:

En la caleta del morillo el Capitan Pedro de Guia del avito de San Juan, con ciento cinquenta soldados	150
En la caleta del cabron, Alonso de Vargas con cien soldados	100
En la puente y boqueron, Pedro Vazquez Alferez con ciento y cinquenta soldados	150
En las fragatas, trecientas personas a orden de Don Pedro Tello	300
En el voca de vayamon, el capitan Otega con cinquenta soldados	50
	750

Toda la demas gente esta en el morro y en la plaça de Armas a cargo del capitan Marco Antonio Veçerra y la de a cavallo al del governador, para acudir los dos cada uno con la de su cargo, a la parte mas combiniente y que mas neçesidas tubiese de socorro.

ARTILLERIA PLANTADA.

En el morro, veinte y siete pieças de bronçe muy buenas	27
En la plata forma del otro morro, çinco pieças	5
En sancta elena, quatro piecas	4
En la caleta de los frayles junto a la fortaleça, tres pieças	3

En la caleta de sancta catalina, çinco pieças	5
En el tejar, nuebe pieças	9
En la boca de vayamon, dos pieças . .	2
En la puente y en un navio que alla se puso, seis pieças.	6
En el boqueron, quatro pieças . . .	4
En la caleta de cabron, dos pieças . .	2
En la caleta del morillo, tres pieças . .	3
	70

y las fragatas bien artilladas; sin las quales avia las dhas setenta pieças de artilleria plantadas y buenos artilleros en cada puesto y por sobreestante de los fuertes del morro y morillo de sancta Elena, el Almirante Gonçalo Mendez de Canço.

A los 15 del dho llego aviso dal governador de Canaria despachado al de aqui, para que supiese como la armada enemiga avia pasado por alli y aviendo echado alguna gente en tierra para haçer agua, le avian echo retirar con daño de veinte y çinco personas, y que venia la buelta de las yndias; y el dho aviso dijo como al pasar por la ysla de san Martin avia visto surta la armada con veinte y çinco velas.

Luego el dho dia el General Sancho Pardo despacho el mismo al governador de la Avana y le escrivio avisase a nueva España al general Pedro Melendez que estava alla con su flota. Estando echas todas estas preventiones toda la gente deseosa de verse con el enemigo, entraron en consejo el dho general y Don Pedro Tello, y el Almirante Gonçalo Mendez y los capitanes Marco Antonio Veçerra, Pedro de Guia, Domingo de Ynsaurraga, el vehedor Martin Vomero de Caamaño, y aviendo tratado si seria bien embarcar la plata en dos fragatas, para que en caso que el enemigo se pusiese sobre el puerto, como mas lijeras se pudiesen escapar de noche, siguiendoles las otras tres en reta guardia, para que si se ofreçiese quedasen peleando y las dos siguiesen su viage;

los mas Votos conformaronse enque no se mudase la plata de donde estava, porque seria desanimar la gente de la tierra que estava con animo de defenderla peleando, y viendo que los desemparavan sedesanimarian y su Magestad perderia la tierra y su reputacion, enque le iba a deçir mucho mas de lo que le importava la plata; que lo que conbenio era haçer rostro al enemigo confiando en Dios que nos daria victoria; y visto por el general la mayor parte de los pareceres, ordeno a Don Pedro Tello que con diligencia aprestase las fragatas, para quando lo estubiese y combiniese embarcar la plata se hiçiese, en el entretanto que el enemigo daria muestras de si por si estubiese esperando al passo, mando fuese una carabela la buelta de la mar 50 leguas a descubrir; y ansi se hiço y la plata se estubo queda que fue bien açertado.

Miercoles 22 del dho mes de Nobiembre al amaneçer se descubrio la armada enemiga a la vista de tierra con 23 velas y una carabela latina, las 6 galeones de la reyna de 800 toneladas, y dos naos del mismo porte y los demas navios de 300, y de 150, y de ayavajo y 40 lanchas venian navegando bien recogidas. Luego se toco a arma y cada qual acudio a su puesto con mucha alegria y buen animo de pelear. El viento era poco y asi venia con espacio asta que entro la briça. Venia delante la carabela latina y algunas lanchas soldando la costa con vanderas blancas en senal, y llegandose una enfrente del boqueron, le tiraron de alli con una pieça que la hiçieron retirar a la mar y luego pusieron otras vanderas coloradas; y pasando delante despues del medio dia, dio fondo toda la armada enfrente de la caleta del cabron donde jamas se vio surgir ningun navio por ser costa y donde no se savia que se podia dar fondo asta despues de ser ydo el enemigo, que embio el general a sondar la parte donde estubo y se allo de 20 a 30 braças en limpio, y segun lo que se entendio era su fin echar alli gente de vajo de su artilleria, pareçiendole allarnos desaperçevidos y que no ubiese ninguna muestra que se le resistiese el paso, y allose engañado.

Estando junta la dha Armada en la parte que digo, los nuestros le tiraron muchas pieças de artilleria del morrillo y de la caleta del cabron, tanto que algunas valas le hiçieron dano por lo que despues que se supo que le mataron a Juan Aquines, general de la una esquadra y a dos caballeros de los principales que con el venian y otra gente, y que a Franº. Draque le llevaron la mesa en que estava comiendo y la bala dio a un personage que con el venia que se supo no escapara.

Viendo el enemigo el dano que de tierra se le haçia, embio la carabela latina con un piloto ysléno de naçion mulato que dicen es muy platico en estas partes, llevando consigo cinco lanchas la buelta del puerto a reconeçerle y a sondar junto la boca del ysloto que llaman ysla de Cabras, que esta a la vanda del oeste, y despues de aver fondado volvio la una lancha a dar aviso a la armada, la qual se desalojo luego de alli a las cinco de la tarde, sin aver tirado pieça ni un solo mosquete en todo el tiempo que alli estubo, y se fue buelta de la mar, y de una y otra se andubo aquella noche asta otro dia.

Juebes siguiente a las ocho de la mañana fue a surgir toda la armada al socayre del yslote que el dia antes avian soldado junto al puerto, que fue otro nuebo surgidero no conoçido asta entonçes por ser fondo de 60 braças sobre bajos subjeto a que con qualquiera tiempo de braveça se pudièra perder en la costa. Alli estubo siendole el tiempo favorable, sin poder la alcançar nuestra artilleria, y aquella tarde embio dos lanchas a asondar la playa de vayamon asta la estacada del carivelo y a reconeçer aquellos vajos para ver si por alli podria echar gente en tierra, y en la una lancha bein entoldada fue Franº. Draque por lo que despues se supo.

Visto por Don Pedro Tello, a cuyo cargo estava el puerto, las diligencias que el enemigo haçia, y pareciendole que avia de acometer por la estacada del carivelo rompiendola aquella noche con lanchas para echar gente en tierra, acudio al general a dar le quenta dello, y a pedirle gente para que fuesen a defender a quel paso, y el general ordeno que aquella tarde estubiese alli el capitan Agustin de Candecho con 30 soldados y que a la noche fuesen 50 soldados a cargo del vehedor Martin Vomero de Caamaño, con orden de que si la fuerça del enemigo fuese superior, se retirase con la gente en los barcos a las fragatas para haçerse fuertes en ellas.

El dicho jueves 23 dia de San Clemente a las 10 de la noche con la obscuridad acometio el enemigo al puerto con 25 lanchas y en cada una de 50 a 60 personas bien armadas con fin de quemar las fragatas segun lo que se vio, y todas entraron arrimadas a la plata forma del morro, metiendose de vajo de la artilleria, y segun lo que despues se supo, Franº. Draque vino en la una asta la boca del puerto, a meter las demas, y aunque hacia obscuro se vieron las lanchas y luego començo a jugar la artilleria del morro y del fuerte de sancta elena y las fragatas muy a priesa, y las mas de las lanchas embistieron con la fragata texeda Capitana poniendole fuego por la proa, echandole dentro muchas alcançias, bombas de fuego, y los nuestros con mucha diligencia lo apagaron sin daño ninguno, peleando con artilleria, mosqueteria, piedras, y al mismo tiempo pusieron fuego a la fragata sancta ysabel y a la fragata Magdalena y a sancta clara, el qual se apago; y la tercera vez que se encendio en la fragata magdalena de que era capitan Domingo de Ynsaurraga, no se pudo apagar, por averse encendido por popa con mucha furia, y todo lo que dio lugar a poder estar en ella y pelear lo hiço el dho capitan y la gente que con el se allo, astaque estava ya casi quemada y muertas 12 personas de la mosqueteria del enemigo, y otras tantas que se quemaron; y el dho capitan se escapo a nado por medio de las lanchas, y se fue a la fragata sancta Ysabel que estava a cargo del capitan Juan Flores de Rabanal en lugar del capitan Pedro de Guia que tenia un sitio de tierra a su cargo, y alli ayudo a todo lo que se ofreçio. Duro el pelear una hora la mas reñida que sea visto, y con el fuego de la fragata que se quemo, aclaro todo el puerto de manera que fue bien para las demas que se veian para asentar nra artilleria y la de los fuertes, con la quel y con la mosqueteria y piedras que de las fragatas se tiraron, les hicieron tanto daño que se retiraron acabo de una ora que como digo se peleava, con perdida de 9 o 10 lanchas y mas de 400 personas sin otros muchos que fueron heridos; no aviendo de nuestra parte mas de la perdida de la fragata y quarenta personas muertas y quemadas, de la mosqueteria algunos heridos. Fue muy de ver lo bien que las fragatas pelearon y quan bien les acudio el artilleria de los fuertes particularmente el de sancta elena que estava mas amano para ofender las lanchas.

Viernes 24, considerando que el enemigo avia de asegundar aquella noche y que avia de echar gente en tierra, dende que amaneçio no çesaron prevençiones por nuestra parte, plantando artilleria en algunos puertos de tierra como fue en todo el tejar, que estava a cargo del governador y del Capitan Marco Antonio con la gente del cuerpo de guardia; en la caleta de sancta Catalina se paso el capitan Guia que antes estava en el morrillo con 50 arcabujeros, y en la caleta de los frayles junto a la fortaleça otros dos pieças y 30 soldados a cargo del vehedor Martin Vomero, y en todas partes se hiçieron muchas trincheras y fortificaçiones trabajando cada qual con el açadon en la mano, sin que hubiese negro que a ello ayudase, porque todos los veçinos los embiaron al monte con sus aciendas y mugeres luego que asomo el enemigo.

Toda via como a las 8 de la mañana con el terral se levo la armada enemiga buelta a la mar procurando ponerse a barlobento del puerto, y ansi andubo asta la tarde y pareçiendole a Don Pedro Tello que esto era para entrarse de golpe en el puerto, fue a tierra a deçirle al general que le pareçia que el enemigo se venia derecho al puerto, y que con los dos naos que se avian echado a fondo, no estava del todo çerrado la canal y que combenia echar dos fragatas en la parte que estava libre para que del todo se ympidiese la entrada, pues era de tanta importancia a segurar el puerto que las dos fragatas por muchas considerationes y bien del serviçio de su Magestad.

El general Sancho Pardo hiço luego junta del governador y de mas ministros, y luego acordaron que se hechase una fragata a fondo en la canal a caso que no bastase un navio de Pedro Sedeño que estava cargado de mercadurias y otro de menos porte, los quales se echasen luego como estavan, pues el brebedad del tiempo no daba lugar a la descarga, y que la fragata se echase quando el dho Don Pedro le pareçiese combenir.

A las 4 de la tarde venia el enemigo con la briça caminando açia el puerto y creyendo Don Pedro Tello que venia derecho a el, echo a fondo los dos navios de Sedeño y Juan Diaz de Sancta Ana, y la fragata tejeda, sin que la brebedad del tiempo diese lugar a sacarle todos los bastimentos y artilleria, aunque alguna parte se saco, y con esto se çerro toda la entrada de la canal, y el enemigo a la oraçion surgio entre el morro y la ysla de cabras donde estubo surto la noche antes.

Visto que la armada estava surta y mas cerca de la entrada del puerto, se volvio a confirmar la sospecha que se tenia de que aquella noche avia de procurar acabar de quemar las fragatas y echar gente en tierra: Don Pedro Tello con acuerdo del general hiço retirar las tres fragatas el puerto adentro, y las metieron en el tejar con gente de guardia por asegurarlas y no temiendo que echasen gente en tierra, viendo quan bien dispuestos estavan los animos de los nuestros y todos los sitios y desembarcaderos atrincherados y fuertes; y el retirar las fragatas fue ya de noche quando el enemigo no lo pudo ver, y ansi el otro dia por la mañana entendio que todas las avia echado a fondo aquella noche, se estubo sosegado sin haçer ninguna demostraçion por nuestra parte si bien estubimos a la mira.

Sabado 25 luego de mañana embio el enemigo siete o ocho lanchas a reconoçer el puerto y toda la costa asta el boqueron, desbiandose de tierra porque nuestra artilleria no los ofendiese y a las 10 de la mañana volvieron a recojerse a la armada que estava junta en la parte dicha.

Este dia a las dos de la tarde asomo nuestra carabela que avia ydo ocho dias antes a descubrir el enemigo, y como por los nuestros fue vista le tiraron una pieça del boqueron para que se recojiese sin yr al puerto, y de la armada le siguieron algunas lanchas asta la playa de cangrejos donde baro y parte de la cavalleria acudio a socorrer la gente, y Fran°. Gonçalez que venia por piloto y capitan de la dha carabela le saco un rumbo porque el enemigo no la llevase y ansi las lanchas se alargaron y se bolvieron sin açer pressa.

El dho sabado en la noche se hiço a la bela toda la armada sin ser vista y se fue a la mar, y viendo los nuestros a la mañana que no parecia, se embio luego personas por tierra prolongando la costa del oeste, para que viesen si pareçia o avia pasado por alli, como se entendia, y yba a Sancto Domingo.

Lunes volvio un aviso del Arracivo catorçe leguas deste puerto, diçiendo que la armada avia pasado por alli su camino adelante. Este dia despacho el governador otro aviso a San German, el qual bolvio dentro de seis dias con nueba de que la armada estava en el butiro de la açucar la otra vanda de San German, y que avia echado en tierra cinco compañias de piqueros y mosqueteros que estavan açiendo carne, agua y leña, y quatro lanchas los quales hiço en quatro dias por traer lo mas echo.

Aviendo el general visto estos avisos y pareçiendole que podria ser odio del enemigo, y que de alli podria ponerse al monte en espera de las dhas fragatas, o querer que fuesen ydas para volver sobre puerto rico por allarle sin fuerça para apoderarse del y executar el designio que traya de fortificarse en el, toco a cuerdo de lo que se aria, y se resolvio que no se saliesen del puerto asta saver de cierto que el enemigo hubiese pasado adelante de la punta de la Aguada, y que fuese el Capitan Juan Flores de Rabanal con un pataje 70 v 80 leguas la buelta del norte a descubrir, y que se embarcase la plata en el entretanto, el qual volvío a cabo de ocho dias sin aver visto nada.

A nueve de diciembre vino aviso de San German que la armada enemiga era yda la buelta del Sur.

A once del dho llego asta çiudad Lope Sanchez contramaestre de la fragata Magdalena y quatro marineros della, que la noche del yncendio de las fragatas los prendieron en el agua las lanchas del enemigo. A los quales echo en tierra en el butrio de la azucar con una carta de Fran° Draque para el governador de aqui, cuya copia es la que sigue;

CARTA de FRAN° DRAQUE A PEDRO SUAREZ CORONEL, governador de Puerto rico;

Entendiendo ser Vs[a] Cavallero prinçipal y soldado escrivo esta breve dando a entender como siempre en todas las ocasiones que semean offreçido con la naçion Española, la e tratado con mucha honora y clemençia, dando libertad a sus personas no apocos mas a muchos, ansi que al tiempo que nuestra gente puso fuego a las fragatas se salvaron ciertos Españoles en la furia del fuego no haçiendo le agravio despues de vençidos sin muy buena guerra.

Por ellos e savido como la capitana de Don Pedro Tello prendio un navichuelo de nuestra armada adonde avia 25 Yngleses, o mas haçiendo con ellos buen tratamiento y guerra limpia. Quedo en el propio ser que solia, mas aviendo otra cosa, forçosamente hase lo que jamas en mi cupo; mas como ay en esa ciudad soldados y cavalleros no dudo del buen suçeso de nuestra gente, dandoles libertad por virtud de buena guerra, lo qual espero y ansi are lo propio; en todo quedo al serviçio de Vs[a], salvo la causa que ay de por medio de la capitana de la sacra Mag[d] de la Reyna de Yngalaterra mis[a]: a 23 Nobiembre de 1595 estilo de Yngalaterra.

FRAN° DRAQUE.

Por relaçion que el dho contramaestre y demas marineros

que ocho dias andubieron con el enemigo, se supo que salieron de alli la buelta del sur o del susudueste, y que yban a Sancto Domingo y de alli a Panama, porque deçian que yban adonde avia mucho oro y plata, y ansi se deja entender por las muchas lanchas que llevaron pertrechos de guerra. Estos çertificaron la muerte de Juan Aquines y el sentimiento que por el se hiço y el mucho daño que los enemigos reçivieron, tanto que pasandolos un dia de la capitana a otro galeon, allaron casi la gente del toda herida y maltratada, y que se quejaban del daño que las piedras que les tiraron de las fragatas les hiço, y que fue tanto el mal que el otro dia de la pelea Fran° Draque hiço consejo sobre si segundaria, no hallo ninguno que fuese de su pareçer, y mas por averles dhos estes hombres que era mucha la fuerça que teniamos mas de la que a sido; y que el Draque se quedo esbentado quando supo la poca gente que se hallo en las fragatas la noche del fuego, y se tiraba de las barbas por no aver tomado la plata y la tierra, no se dejando ver aquellos dos dias, quejandose de Juan Aquines que no quiso que vineran tras las fragatas de la ysla de Guadalupe luego que supo que le avian cojido el navio y venian a puerto rico, dando a entender que no tubieramos lugar de fortificarmos como se hiço en los ocho dias que se tardaron en aprestar sus lanchas y en haçer agua. Todo lo a ordenado Dios a quien se debe dar muchas graçias, pues mediante su labor de mas de aver alcançado una victoria tel, con tan poca gente como de nuestra parte hubo resistiendo la fuerça de una armada tan poderosa, defendiendo la tierra y dos millones de plata, a su Magestad selea seguido notables serviçios y a los particulares bien general.

Lo primero, que por lo que sea entendido el enemigo traya fin de sustentar esta fuerça y fuera le facil con poca costa, porque los cosarios que andan en esto de todas naçiones seacojieran a ella y ellos ayudara a defenderla, y fuera menester armar muy de proposito para bolverse la a ganar, por ser el serviçio del puerto fuerte y de donde mas daño pueden haçer a yslotas y costas que todo lo tiene a sotavento.

Lo segundo, que a este enemigo, que asta oy nadie lea echo resistençia en la mar, aqui se le rompio la caveça, pues como esta dho, una de las dos que governaban murio y 400 personas y hubo muchos heridos.

Lo 3, que se escaparon dos millones de plata y oro y granas con que la Reyna podia armar y entretenerse por mas ynquietar nos.

Lo 4, que con averse entretenido en estas yslas asta los 3 de Diçiembre, dio tiempo a que sepuedan aver prevenido los lugares sospechosos con los avisos que esta dho sedespacharon a Sancto Domingo y a la avana, y destos los avian tenido en Cartagena y nueba espana con que podemos esperar seguridad.

Lo ultimo, y no demenos consideraçion es el animo y reputaçion que los nuestros an cobrado, reconoçiendo el poco valor de los enemigos, y por el contrario la opinion que ellos an perdido, en que consiste mucha parte de los buenos o malos subçesos, y pues desta se siguen tantos viénes, su Magestad debe haçer merced a los que en el se allaron para que los que estan a la mira se animen a servirle en semeyantes ocasiones.

Pasada esta como esta dho, y aviendo el general tenido aviso que el enemigo yba adelante, y que los vastimentos eran pocos por averse gastado muchos en esta ocasion, y ser la miseria desta ysla tal que no se podian proveer otros, y que combenia abreviar la partida de sudespacho, y ordeno que con suma presteça se recojiese el artilleria de los puestos de tierra y se embarcase la plata en los fragatas, y con ellas y con un navio y un patache en que se embarco parte de la gente y artilleria de las dos fragatas perdidas y de la capitana de tierra firme, partio de puerto rico con buen tiempo a los 20 de Diçiembre de 1595.

INSTRUCCION que dio Fran°. Draque, al capitan del navio Françes, uno de los de su armada que se le tomo en la ysla de Guadalupe.

La instrucçion y orden que a de tener toda la armada que sale del puerto de Plemua desde 29 de Agosto de 1595 años.

1. Primeramente es para servir a Dios y tener esta orden dos veçes aldia y sino fuese alguna ocasion no poder mas.

2. Lo segundo aveis de tener gran cuidado de tener compania y venir a hablar a vuestro Almirante dos veçes aldia, y quando no pudieredes mas de una vez, lo haçed cada dia y tened gran cuidado de la orden que vos sera dada de guardarla y tener siempre estar en compania como el tiempo ordenare.

3. Y si fuese algun navio o patache per tempestad de tiempo o per otra ocasion que hubiese y se apartase de la compania anos de allar primeramente en la ysla de Bayona de Galicia y alli estara la armada aguardando asta que el tiempo provea otra cosa y nos allareis, y de alli sino nos allaredes, yreis a Puerto Sancto y nos aguardareis alli tres dias, y sino fueremos alli, tomareis el camino para la ysla de Guadalupe, una ysla pequena de la vanda del nordeste çerca de la Dominica, en la qual estaremos tres dias y dejaremos alguna sinal para que sepais donde nosotros fueremos el qual sera para puerto rico; alli estaremos diez dias.

4. Si en este camino tubieremos algun viento contrario e tempestad de noche, aveis de amaynar todas los belas asta la mañana, sino vieredes que una almiranta aga bela y ansi areis vosotros lo mismo.

5. Y si el tiempo volviese de noche alguna contrariedad de vento contrario, vuestra almiranta pondra dos lanternas, una de vajo de otra de statura de un hombre, para que os vais regiendo por ellas.

6. Y si todos nosotros amaynasemos de noche por alguna ocasion de tempestad y fuese neçesario haçer vela esa noche,

aveis de ençender antes que nosotros echemos vela una sola lanterna con lumbre en popa y otra en la gavia del trinquete.

7. No tendreis ninguna lumbre en ningun navio sino solamente la lumbre que estubiese en la aguia, y este con gran cuydado que no pareçia, fuera de la Almiranta y por los ocasiones que pueden venir del fuego, no aveis de traer ninguna candela ni lumbre entorno del navio sino fuese con lanterna, y ni mas ni menos aveis de tener gran cuidado con el fuego de la coçina.

8. Ningun navio baral ni patache no vaya delante de la Almirante de noche y particularmente en tiempo de fortuna de tempestad ni se ponga de vajo de los navios grandes pasando de una parte a otra.

9. Y si algun navio de la flota por desgraçia perdiese algun arbol mayor o verga o alguna bomba o otro aparejo alguno de importançia, tiraran una v dos pieças conforme a la necesitad que tubiese para que los otros navios le socorran con brevedad, y que ningun navio se aparte della asta que se socorra, conforme a la necesitad que se tubiese.

10. Y si algun navio de la flota perdiese su curso y topase con otro algun navio, la señal sera que içaran y amaynaran la vela de gavia tres veçes y ansi ara la otra para que se conosca.

11. No aveis de consentir jugar en el navio naypos ni dados por muchas ocasiones que suelen suçeder de pendençias.

12. Aveis de tener grandissimo cuydado de conservar los bastimentos, conforme a vuestra discreçion asta que reçivais otra orden de lo que aveis de haçer.

13. Lo ultimo para que agais mejor compañia, vereis una lumbre en la popa Almiranta una o dos veçes.

FRAN^o^. DRAQUE.

AN ACCOUNT OF WHAT TOOK PLACE AT SAN JUAN DE PUERTO RICO, IN THE INDIES, WITH THE ENGLISH FLEET UNDER THE COMMAND OF FRANCIS DRAKE AND JOHN HAWKINS, ON THE 23RD NOVEMBER 1595.

(The Translation of the preceding document.)

GENERAL Sancho Pardo y Osorio having taken his departure from the Havana for Spain on the 10th March of this year, in command of the Capitana of the main-land fleet, under convoy of the armed fleet of Don Francisco de Coloma, and having, in the course of the gale which blew in the chops of the Channel on the 15th of the same month, in latitude 23° 30′, found himself without a main-mast, and with tiller broken, while the ship, leaking much, and separated from the others, was no longer in a condition to prosecute the voyage, for the purpose of saving the lives of the three hundred people who were on board, as well as two millions of gold and silver belonging to His Majesty and to private individuals; with the advice and consent of the supercargo, Martin Vomero de Caamaño, and of the pilots and other persons of most experience on board, made for Puerto Rico, where he arrived, by a miracle, on the 9th April, and there he landed the bullion, and deposited it in the fortress of the town. The aforesaid general despatched immediately first and second advices to His Majesty, making known his arrival, in order that instructions might be sent to him as to what he should do. And it appears that Divine Providence (to whom many thanks are due), for its secret ends, permitted the orders, which might have come beforehand, to arrive just at the time to save not only the bullion, but the island itself, and perhaps all the Indies, as will be seen further on.

A few days after the aforesaid letters were despatched, the governor of this island, Colonel Pedro Suares, received those of His Majesty, whereby he was informed that a great fleet was fitting out in England for the purpose of seizing on this island in the course of the winter, as it was thought that at that season the inhabitants would be less upon their guard. When the general and the aforesaid supercargo learned the contents of these despatches, they joined in consultation with the governor and Francisco Cid, captain of the infantry of this garrison; and having taken into consideration and discussed the precautionary measures which ought to be adopted for the safety of the place and of His Majesty's treasure, in order that, if the enemy should come, it might be out of his power to make himself master of the whole, they all agreed on reconnoitering the positions and accessible points from which the enemy might approach, so as to throw people ashore; and also that the general should give orders for planting some of the guns of his ship in the positions which he judged best, and for laying the vessel athwart the channel of the port, so that she might be sunk on the arrival of the enemy, and thus bar the entrance; as this was the quarter where there seemed most likelihood of attack and most risk, and where it was necessary to keep the people well on the watch. These arrangements being made, the general remained in expectation of His Majesty's order to proceed on his voyage.

On the 13th November of this year, there arrived at this port, Don Pedro Tello de Guzman, with the five frigates of His Majesty, in order that General Sancho Pardo should embark in them His Majesty's bullion, and so proceed to Spain, the post of Admiral of his fleet being filled by the aforesaid Pedro Tello, who, after having delivered his despatches, related to the aforesaid general, how, coming here in the course of his voyage, they had fallen in with two English ships at the island of Guadaloupe, which had parted company from the English fleet; and how his Admiral, Gonzalo Mendez de Canço, had captured one of them and sunk her, after taking the Englishmen out of her; and that he, the aforesaid Don Pedro, going in pursuit of the other vessel, discovered nine sail of the enemy's fleet, and as soon as he descried them he tacked about and continued his voyage: and that the aforesaid English prisoners had stated that thereabouts, on the southern side of the island of Guadaloupe, the Queen of England's fleet was lying at anchor and preparing launches; that it consisted of five-and-twenty ships, six of them Queen's galleons of eight hundred tons burden, and two more of the same size belonging to private parties, the whole being divided into two squadrons, having for generals, Francis Drake and John Hawkins; the former, with his lieutenant in command on shore, Sir Thomas Baskerville, directing the course to be taken, and the proceedings on land; and that the armament amounted to three thousand infantry and ten thousand five hundred seamen well supplied with guns; and that they were coming direct to Puerto Rico, as appeared also from the instructions which were taken from the captain of the aforesaid English ship, in which he was ordered, in case he should part company from the fleet by any mischance, to proceed to Puerto Rico, where they would wait for him ten days, and after that, would leave orders for him where he was to go, without further revealing their intentions; and that in consequence of all this, the aforesaid Don Pedro came, fearing that the enemy might have preceded him and already got possession of the island; and since they had not yet come, he held it for certain that they would be down upon the port the next day; and accordingly it lay with the general to order his departure as it might seem expedient.

When the general, Sancho Pardo, heard the statement

made by the aforesaid Don Pedro Tello and his admiral, Gonzalo Mendez; and inasmuch as that news reached him when he was confined to his bed by an illness under which he had been suffering some days, he sent word to the Bishop and to the Governor, requesting them to come to him to meet the captains of the frigates,—Marco Antonio Becerra, head of the company of fusileers; and Pedro de Guia, of the order of St. John; and Domingo de Ynsaurraga; Francisco Gomez, captain of this garrison; the supercargo, Martin Vomero de Caamaño, and Juan de la Vera, purser of the frigates. These having all met together in his house, the general laid before them and submitted for their consideration the account which he had of the enemy, and the best means that offered for the security of the island and the bullion, supposing that the enemy's fleet was as great, and to be expected as soon as was said; and that the frigates absolutely required to have their rigging repaired and to take in wood and water, which, with embarking the bullion, would cause a delay of eight days at the least; and considering that, whether they were so occupied or not, the enemy by reason of the information which that other ship that was seen could give him, that these frigates were coming for the treasure, which was now known to be here, might hope to seize it on the passage, or to make himself master of the country and to fortify himself in it, with a view to the conquest of all the Indies, whence would ensue to His Majesty great injury and loss of reputation.

All were of one mind in thinking that the place ought to be strengthened with the guns and crews of the ships, and that the Capitana de Tierra Firme and another ship belonging to Pedro Milanes, should be sunk in the channel of the port, to shut the entrance, and that the bullion should not be moved from the fort until it was seen what turn affairs would take, as it appeared to be safer there, and in a position also, whence (if, for our sins, it should be so ordered) it might be more easily thrown into the sea, so that the enemy should not get it; and having thus resolved, they proceeded to carry into execution with great alacrity and zeal, night and dry, every possible measure of defence.

General Sancho Pardo, as a person of great experience, and who had seen and examined the position and approaches of the place, assured Don Pedro Tello and the others who came with him, that the loss of the place was out of the question if our people were only willing to fight and do their duty, and that it was only necessary to take good care of the port, so as to prevent the enemy's fleet running into it at once; and that, for that purpose, it were as well to sink the two ships which had been agreed on, and on top of them, the frigates with their bows towards the sea to bar the entrance, and that with this precaution the place was quite safe and also the treasure of His Majesty, who, herein, would be well served, and in whose name he called on them to attend to their several duties; and accordingly Don Pedro Tello took under his own charge the defence of the port.

The Bishop offered to say mass the next day, and to preach a sermon to the people, as he did in fact, exhorting them, in a Christian manner, to the service of God and of their king; and he persevered in the performance of this office night and day, visiting the posts where the people were stationed, placing a priest at each of them, and animating his hearers with much zeal.

The same day, the governor and general despatched a barque with advices to St. Domingo, that the inhabitants of that island might set and keep themselves on the watch; so that if the enemy were to go there, as was heard and was written to the President, the information might be immediately forwarded to Cartagena and Sancta Maria.

All the people of the island were immediately mustered, and some of those belonging to the frigates were landed, being thought necessary for the defence of the posts. The whole amounted to ten thousand three hundred souls, of whom seven hundred were fighting men, besides the eight hundred belonging to the frigates and the Capitana of the mainland, and the rest of the garrison, and foreigners, including, also, fifty on horseback with lance and buckler; the whole of whom were distributed in the following manner:

In the curtain of the Morillo [battery], Captain Pedro de Guia, of the order of St. John, with a hundred and fifty soldiers .	150
In the curtain of the Cabron, Alonso de Vargas with a hundred soldiers . .	100
At the bridge and Boqueron, Ensign Pedro Vazquez with a hundred and fifty soldiers	150
In the frigates, three hundred men under the command of Don Pedro Tello . .	300
At the mouth of the river Bayamon, Captain Otega with fifty soldiers . .	50
	750

The rest of the people occupied the Morro and the esplanade, under the command of Captain Marco Antonio de Veçerra and the governor, who led the cavalry; each of them to advance with his party to whatever point seemed to require his presence, or to stand in need of succour.

ARTILLERY PLANTED.

On the Morro [rock battery], twenty-seven very good brass guns	27
On the platform of the other Morro, five pieces	5
In St. Helena, four pieces	4
In the curtain of the Friars, close to the fortress, three pieces	3
In the curtain of St. Catharine, five pieces	5
In the Tejar [tile field], nine pieces . .	9
At the mouth of the river, two pieces .	2

On the bridge and in a ship which was placed there, six pieces	6
On the Boqueron, four pieces . . .	4
On the Cabron curtain, two pieces . .	2
On the curtain of the Morillo, three pieces	3
	70

Besides the frigates well armed, without which there were the aforesaid seventy pieces of cannon planted with good gunners at each post, and for chief commander of the forts of the Morro and the Morillo de Sta. Helena, the Admiral, Gonçalo Mendez de Canço.

On the 15th of the same month intelligence arrived from the governor of Canary, despatched to the governor of this island, to make it known that the enemy's fleet had passed by the former place, and having landed some people for the purpose of watering, they had been forced to retreat with the loss of five-and-twenty men, and had gone off towards the Indies; and the same messenger stated, that in passing by the island of St. Martin, he had seen the armada, of five-and-twenty sail, lying at anchor.

Immediately, on the same day, the general, Sancho Pardo, sent the same despatch to the governor of the Havana, and wrote to him to forward the information to New Spain to General Pedro Melendez, who was on that coast with his fleet. These precautionary steps having been taken, and the people being all eager to combat the enemy, the general held a council, at which were present, Don Pedro Tello; the admiral, Gonçalo Mendez; and the captains, Marco Antonio Veçerra, Pedro de Guia, and Domingo de Ynsaurraga, with the supercargo Martin Vomero de Caamaño; and having taken into consideration whether it were expedient to embark the bullion in two of the frigates, so that if the enemy should place himself before the port, these being lighter, might effect their escape by night, the other three following them in the rear, in order that, if any attempt were made upon them, they might stay behind fighting while the two continued their voyage; it was decided by the majority of votes, that the bullion should not be removed from the place where it was lying, because the removal of it would tend to dispirit the people, who were fired with the thought of defending it: seeing their expectations foiled, they would be dispirited, and His Majesty would lose the place and his reputation, which was to be valued much more highly than the bullion: and what it behoved them to do, was to face the enemy, trusting in God for the victory. When the general saw how the majority inclined, he gave orders to Don Pedro Tello to get the frigates ready with all convenient despatch, that the bullion might be embarked whenever it was found expedient to do so; the enemy, it was supposed, would afford indications of his intentions, if he had such, of watching for it outside; and he directed that a caravel should cruise on the look out, about fifty leagues off the land. This was done accordingly, and the bullion remained as it was, which was the prudent course.

Wednesday the 22nd of the same month (November), at break of day, the enemy's fleet was descried on the horizon, with twenty-three sail and a pinnace. The six queen's galleons of eight hundred tons, and two ships of the same size, and the rest, vessels of three hundred tons and of one hundred and fifty and less, and forty launches, came sailing in close order. Immediately every one snatched up his arms and ran to his post with great alacrity, and well disposed for combat. There was but little wind, and so the fleet advanced but slowly till it entered the breeze. The pinnace came first and some boats with white signal-flags sounding the coast. One of them having come in front of the Boqueron battery, a gun was fired at it which made it stand off to sea, and they immediately hoisted other coloured flags and passed out; and in the afternoon the whole fleet came and cast anchor in front of the curtain of the Cabron, where no one had ever seen a ship ride before, nor was it known that there was good anchorage till after the departure of the enemy, when the general sent to have the place sounded, and from twenty to thirty fathoms clear water were found there. From what was learned, it appears to have been his intention to land a force under the fire of his artillery, imagining that he should find us unprepared, and seeing no reason to believe that such a step would meet with resistance; wherein he was mistaken.

The fleet having arrived in the place above-mentioned, our people fired at it several pieces of artillery from the Morrillo and the curtain of the Cabron, so that some of the shot took effect on them, for it was known afterwards, that they killed John Hawkins, the general of one of the squadrons, and two of the principal gentlemen who accompanied him, besides other people; and that they carried away the table at which Francis Drake was eating, the ball striking a gentleman who was with him, and who, it is known, will not escape.

The enemy perceiving how much loss he sustained from the shore, sent the pinnace with a pilot, a native of the islands and a mulatto by race, who is said to be practically well acquainted with these coasts, with five boats to the port, to reconnoitre it and to sound close to the mouth formed by the islet, which is called Goat Island, which lies towards the west; and when it was sounded, one of the boats returned with information to the fleet, which immediately weighed anchor, at five o'clock in the evening, without having fired a cannon or even a musket during all the whole time that it was there, and ran out to sea, where it stood off and on that night till the following day.

Thursday following, at eight o'clock in the morning, the whole fleet came and anchored on the windward side of the small island where they had been sounding the day before, close to the port; and this was another new anchorage not known hitherto, and having six fathoms over shoals, where a vessel might be easily lost in any bad weather. There the fleet anchored, the weather being favourable, and beyond the reach of our artillery; and the same evening two boats were sent to sound the shore by the river Bayamon as far as the Carivelo stockade, and to examine these shoals in order to see if it were possible to land a force in that quarter; and in one of the boats, which was covered closely with an awning, was Francis Drake, as was subsequently learned.

When Don Pedro Tello, who had charge of the port, saw the pains the enemy was taking, and perceived that an attack was about to be made that very night on the stockade of the Carivelo, by forcing it with boats, so as to land a body of men, he sent to the general to acquaint him with what was going on, and to ask for a reinforcement to resist such an attempt; and the general ordered that in the evening Captain Augustin de Candecho should proceed thither with thirty soldiers, and that at night there should be fifty soldiers under the command of the supercargo, Martin Vomero de Caamaño, with orders that if the enemy's force should prove superior, he should retreat with his men in boats to the frigates, in which their forces were to be concentrated.

The same Thursday, 23rd, St. Clement's day, at ten o'clock at night, when it was quite dark, the enemy commenced an attack on the port with twenty-five boats, each carrying fifty or sixty men well armed, with the view of burning the frigates, as was afterwards seen, and they all entered close up to the platform of the Rock [battery], ranging themselves under the fire of the artillery; and from what was learned afterwards, it appears that Francis Drake came in one of them to the mouth of the port to place the rest. Dark as it was, the boats were seen, and instantly the guns from the Rock and from the fort of Sta. Helena began to play as briskly as possible. Most of the boats attacked the Capitana, the Texeda frigate, setting fire to her at the bow, and throwing into her a quantity of fire-pots and shells, while ours succeeded in extinguishing the flames before they had done any damage, the fight being carried on with cannon, musquetry, and stones.

At the same time they set fire to the Sta. Ysabel and Magdalena frigates, and to the Sancta Clara, which was extinguished; but the third time that the Magdalena frigate, of which Domingo de Ynsaurraga was captain, took fire, it was impossible to extinguish the flames, as the ship took fire at the stern and burned furiously; and all that could be done to maintain a footing on board, was done by the aforesaid captain and the people with him, until the ship was just burnt down and twelve men were killed by the enemy's musquetry, besides as many more burnt. And the aforesaid captain made his escape by swimming through the midst of the boats and reached the frigate Sancta Ysabel, which was under the command of Captain Juan Flores de Rabanal in place of Captain Pedro de Guia, who had charge of a post on land, and there he lent his assistance in every manner possible. The battle lasted for an hour, the most obstinately contested that was ever seen, and the whole port was illumined by the burning frigate in a manner favourable for the rest, who could thus see to point our artillery and that of the forts, with which, and with the musquetry and the stones thrown from the frigate, they did such effect, that the enemy, after about an hour, during which the combat lasted, as I have said, retreated with the loss of nine or ten boats and more than four hundred men, besides many more wounded; while on our side, the only loss was that of the frigate and forty men killed or burnt, besides a few wounded by the musquetry. It was a fine sight to see how the frigates fought, and how capitally they were backed by the artillery of the forts, particularly that of Sta. Helena, which was in an advantageous position for playing on the boats.

Friday 24th. Considering that the enemy would assuredly

repeat his attack at night, and endeavour to land his forces, the people on our side never ceased, from the dawn of day, to prepare for resistance, planting cannon at some passes on land, as was done, for example, in the whole of the Tejar, where the governor commanded, with Captain Marco Antonio and the people forming the company of guards. Captain Guia, who previously kept guard in the Morrillo, now took his station in the curtain of Sancta Catalina with fifty arquebusseers; in the curtain of the Friars, close to the fortress, were two other pieces with thirty soldiers, under the command of the supercargo, Martin Vomero, and on every side numerous trenches were dug and defences constructed, every one working spade in hand, and not a single negro to assist, for the people round about had sent off all their slaves to the mountain, with their effects and women, as soon as the enemy appeared.

However, about eight o'clock in the morning, as soon as the land breeze sprang up, the enemy's fleet weighed and stood to sea, endeavouring to get to windward of the port, and continued on this course till evening; and Don Pedro Tello perceiving that the object was to run at once into the port, went ashore to explain to the general his apprehension that the enemy was about to bear down directly on the place: that the two ships which had been already sunk did not completely close up the entrance to it, and that it was expedient to sink two frigates in the part that still remained open, inasmuch as the complete barring of the entrance and the security of the port were quite as important as the two frigates, for many reasons, and for the good of His Majesty's service.

General Sancho Pardo immediately held a council with the governor and other officers, and they decided that one frigate should be sunk in the channel, in case that a ship belonging to Pedro Sedeño, which was lying there laden with merchandise, and another of less size, should prove insufficient; that these should be sunk immediately, just as they were, as there was not time to unload them, and that the frigate should be sunk whenever Don Pedro thought proper.

At four o'clock in the afternoon the enemy came running down with the breeze towards the port, and Don Pedro Tello, believing that he was making directly for it, sank the two vessels of Sedeño and Juan Diaz de Sancta Aña, and also the Texeda frigate, without being able, owing to the short time allowed, to take out of them all the provisions and guns, although a part was saved; and thus the entrance of the channel was completely closed, and about vesper time the enemy came to anchor between the Rock and Goat island, where he had lain at anchor the night before.

The circumstance that the fleet anchored, and nearer than before to the port, tended to confirm the suspicion that the enemy meant to attempt that very night to finish the burning of the frigates, and to land people. Don Pedro Tello, therefore, with the consent of the governor, had the three frigates brought back to the interior of the port, and they were placed in the Tejar with a guard to secure them; but he had no fears about the landing of a force, seeing the spirit which animated our people, and that all the posts and landing-places were well entrenched and strengthened. The removal of the frigates took place at night, when the enemy could see nothing, and consequently the next morning he concluded that they had been all sunk. The night passed off quietly, without any effort on our part to shew that we were well on the watch.

Saturday the 25th, as soon as daylight appeared, the enemy sent seven or eight boats to reconnoitre the port, and all the shore as far as the Boqueron. These kept at a distance from land, beyond the reach of our guns; and about ten o'clock they returned to the fleet, which remained at anchor in the place above-mentioned.

The same day, about two o'clock in the afternoon, our caravel, which had gone to look out for the enemy eight days before, came in sight, and as soon as it was seen by our people, they fired a gun from the Boqueron to warn it to bear up without approaching the port; and some boats from the fleet followed it as far as the Playa de Cangrejos (crab ground), where it ran ashore, and part of the cavalry hastened forward to assist the crew; and Francisco Gonçalez, who was the pilot and captain of the caravel, scuttled her, to prevent the enemy's carrying her off; and so the boats went away, and returned to the fleet without making a prize.

The same Saturday, at night, the whole fleet made sail without being seen, and stood out to sea; and when we found in the morning that it had disappeared, people were sent by land westwards along the coast to ascertain whether it was seen or had passed that way, as was supposed, and was going to St. Domingo.

On Monday news arrived from Arracibo, fourteen leagues from this port, that the fleet had passed by on its course. The same day the general despatched another messenger to San German, who returned within six days with the information that the enemy's fleet was lying in the Butiro de la Azucar on the other side of San German, and that they had landed five companies of pikemen and musqueteers, who were collecting supplies of meat, wood, and water, and made four boats in as many days to carry their supplies.

The general having received this intelligence, and thinking it likely that there might be some artifice in the enemy's movements, who perhaps might be lying in wait hoping to catch the two frigates, or intending to return upon Puerto Rico when they should be gone and the place weakened, in order that he might seize it, and execute his design of fortifying himself in it, seriously deliberated as to what should be done, and determined that the frigates should not quit the port till it was known for certain that the enemy had passed Point de la Aguada; and that Captain Juan Flores de Rabanal should go seventy or eighty leagues to the north with a patache to look out, while the bullion was in the meantime embarking. In eight days he returned, without having seen anything.

The 9th of December intelligence was brought from San German that the enemy's fleet had gone away southwards.

On the 11th of the same month there arrived at this place Lope Sanchez, boatswain of the Magdalena frigate, and four seamen of the same, who had been taken in the water by the enemy's boats, the night the frigates were set on fire. These men had been put on shore in the Butiro de la Azucar, with a letter of Francis Drake to the governor here, of which the following is a copy:—

Letter of Francis Drake to Colonel Pedro Suarez, Governor of Puerto Rico.

"Understanding that your lordship is a gentleman of rank and a soldier, I write this letter to give you to understand that whenever I have had an opportunity of dealing with the Spanish nation, I have treated it with much honour and clemency, liberating the individuals belonging to it, not a few, but many in number. So, at the time when our people set fire to the frigates, certain Spaniards were saved from the fury of the flames, who, as conquered enemies, experienced from us no ill-treatment, but the usage of honourable war.

"From them it has been learned that the capitana of Don Pedro Tello took a small vessel of our fleet, having on board twenty-five Englishmen, or more, treating them well, and as might be expected in fair war. I myself still cherish my former sentiments; but having another affair, strong deeds are done, which never entered my mind. But as there are in this place soldiers and gentlemen, I have no doubt that my people will fare well, and will obtain their liberty for the sake of honourable war: this I hope, and shall do the like myself. I remain at your lordship's service in all things, bating the cause which is to be maintained as that of the flag of her sacred Majesty the queen of England.

"FRANCIS DRAKE.

"The 23d November 1595, English style."

From the information given by the aforesaid boatswain and the other seamen, who had gone with the enemy for eight days, it was ascertained that the latter had departed thence towards the S. or S.S.W., and that they were going to St. Domingo and thence to Panama, for they said that they were going where there was a quantity of gold and silver; and the same thing might also be inferred from the number of boats they took with them for an armament.

These men confirmed also the death of John Hawkins, and testified as to the regret occasioned thereby, as well as to the heavy loss which the enemy sustained. Thus, as a boat was passing one day from the flag-ship to one of the other galleons, it was struck, and nearly every man in it was wounded. They stated that the enemy complained much of the damage done by the stones thrown from the frigates; and that the loss was so great, that when Francis Drake held a council the day after the battle, to determine whether they should renew the attack, there was not one who agreed with him in favour of that proposition, especially as these men had told them that our force was much greater than it used to be; and that Drake was amazed when he learned how few people were on board of the frigates the night of the fire, and plucked his beard [with vexation] for not having taken the treasure and the place, not letting himself be seen those two days; complaining of John Hawkins, who did not allow them to pursue the three frigates from the island of Guadaloupe, as soon as it was known that they had taken the vessel and were making for Puerto Rico; intimating that in that case we should not have had the opportunity of fortifying the place, as was done in the eight days which they spent in the delay of preparing boats, and watering.

All this has been so ordered by God, to whom we owe many thanks, since by His means, besides obtaining such a victory, with so small a force as that which on our side resisted the efforts of so powerful an armament, in defence of the place and two millions of treasure, important services have resulted to his Majesty, and a general gain to private individuals.

In the first place, as far as can be learned, it was the enemy's intention to maintain this force, which he might easily do at small cost, for the pirates of all nations who frequent these seas, would gather about him, and would aid him in defending the position; and it would then be necessary to fit out an expedition expressly to retake the place, since the port has a decided advantage, and from thence much injury may be easily done to the islands and coasts which are to leeward.

In the second place, this enemy, who up to this time has never met with any resistance at sea, has here had his head broken; since, as has been related, one of the two leaders died, with four hundred of his followers, and a great many were wounded.

Thirdly, we have thus saved two millions worth of gold, silver, and cochineal, with which the queen might equip and maintain a force to give us further trouble.

Fourthly, the delaying of the enemy in these islands till the 3rd December, allowed time for warning those places for the safety of which fears might be entertained, by means of the despatches which were sent, as has been stated, to St. Domingo and the Havana, whence others were forwarded to Carthagena and New Spain, so that we may now hope that all is safe.

The last, and not the least consideration, is, the spirit which our people have shewn, and the renown which they have won, proving the inferiority of the enemy; and, on the other hand, the hold on opinion which the latter have lost, and in which consists to a great extent the secret of good or ill-success. And since the beneficial results of this affair are so many, his Majesty ought to return thanks to those who took part in it, in order that the lookers-on may be encouraged to serve him on like occasions.

This affair having passed over as here related, and the general having received information that the enemy was gone on, and that provisions were scarce, a quantity of them having been lost on this occasion, and the poverty of the island being such that the deficiency could not be made good, and that it was necessary for him to abridge his delay as much as possible, gave orders to collect the guns with the utmost despatch from the several posts on land, and to embark the treasure in the frigates; and with these, one ship, and a patache, in which were embarked part of the crews and artillery of the two lost frigates, he left Puerto Rico with good weather on the 20th December 1595.

The INSTRUCTIONS given by F. Drake to the captain of the Francis, one of the vessels of his fleet, which was taken at the island of Guadaloupe.

The Instruction and Order to be observed by the whole fleet, which departs from the port of Plymouth on the 29th August 1595.

1. In the first place, omit not divine worship, and let this order be observed twice a-day, unless no opportunity offers.

2. Secondly, great care must be taken to keep company and to come to speak with your admiral twice a-day; and if you cannot do it more than once, yet let it be done every day; and take great care to observe every order given you, and to be always in company, as the weather shall allow.

3. And should it happen that any ship or small vessel, through stress of weather or other cause that may be, parts company, they must look for us first of all in the island of Bayona, on the coast of Galicia, and the fleet will wait till it is time to proceed and you shall have found us; and thence, if you should not find us, you shall go to Puerto Sancto, and there you shall wait for us three days; and should we not be there, you shall make for the island of Guadaloupe (a small island near Dominica towards the north-east), where we will stay three days, and will leave some signal that you may know what course we shall have taken, which shall be for Puerto Rico; there we will stay ten days.

4. If in the course of this voyage you meet with any foul wind or bad weather, you must take in all sail at night till morning, unless you see that one of your admirals carries sail, in which case you shall do the same.

5. And if foul wind or bad weather should come on at night, your admiral will hang out two lanterns, one above the other, and the height of a man asunder, that you may steer by them.

6. And if we should all shorten sail over night on account of the weather, and it be necessary to make sail the same night, you must show, before we make sail, a single lantern with a light at the bow, and another at the fore-top.

7. You shall keep no light in any of the ships, but only the light in the binocle, and this with the greatest care that it be not seen, excepting the admiral's ship; and to avoid the danger of fire, you must not bear about any candle or light in the ship, unless in a lantern; and neither more nor less, you must take the greatest care with the fire in the galley.

8. No vessel, square or cutter-rigged, should go a-head of the admiral at night, particularly in rough weather; or get under the lee of large vessels, in tacking from side to side.

9. And if any vessel of the fleet should lose, through mischance, a mainmast, or yard, or any of the water vessels, or anything else of importance, they shall fire one or two shots, according to the necessity of the case, that the other vessels may afford them speedy assistance; and take care that no vessel quit that which is in distress till the required succour be given.

10. Should any vessel of the fleet lose her course, and fall in with another of the fleet, the signal shall be to hoist and lower topsails three times; and the other vessel shall do the same for recognition.

11. You must not permit any gambling in the ship, with cards or dice, by reason of the numerous quarrels usually resulting from that practice.

12. You must take the greatest care to save the provisions, following your own discretion in this matter till you receive another order for your guidance.

13. Finally, in order that you may be better able to keep company, you shall see a light at the admiral's stern once or twice.

FRANCIS DRAKE.

FINIS.

RICHARDS, PRINTER,
100, ST. MARTIN'S LANE.

Lightning Source UK Ltd.
Milton Keynes UK
02 November 2010

162239UK00001B/38/P